INVESTING
3.0

INVESTING 3.0

**WHAT THE CREATORS OF INDEX FUNDS
DISCOVERED AND HOW TO PROFIT FROM IT**

Richard A. Raybin

Published by Lifetime Capital Group, LLC, San Mateo, California
2017

Lifetime Capital Group, LLC
50 Mounds Road
San Mateo, CA 94402
www.lifetimecapitalgroup.com

Ordering Information:
Individual sales. This book is available through Amazon.com and other online and brick-and-mortar bookstores.
Quantity sales. Special discounts are available on quantity purchases by corporations, associations, and others. For details, contact the publisher at the address above.
Financial advisors. Special order books with a customized forward are available. Contact the editor above for information.

ISBN: 0692952896
ISBN 13: 9780692952894
Printed in the United States of America

First Edition

TABLE OF CONTENTS

INTRODUCTION

M any investors have been so disillusioned by the performance of stockbrokers, investment advisors, and *mutual funds* (see the "Glossary" for more in-depth definitions of terms displayed in *bold italics*) that, for better or worse, they make their own investment decisions. Some rely on reading or watching the financial news or studying company financial data to identify individual companies that will do well. Some pick mutual funds based on the name or *performance* over the last one, three, and five years, cross their fingers, and hope for the best.

If you're feeling disappointed, confused, or frustrated by all the conflicting "advice", you need to know you are not alone. In fact, experiences like yours spurred economists to develop the academic field of finance. And, as they searched for insights, they discovered a better way to invest. Just as scientific research has led to advances in medicine and computers, financial market research has led to major advances in investing, such as the launch of *index funds*. Since their introduction in the 1970s, the performance of index funds has surpassed the performance of Wall Street's traditional methods of investing. Now, more recent advances are surpassing the performance of index funds!

If you want to understand the advances discovered after index funds were introduced, what led to them, and how you can profit from them, then keep reading!

Investing—The Search for Knowledge

To most of us, the financial world can feel like a massive Tower of Babel, with thousands of people speaking languages we can't understand, selling products we don't know how to evaluate, with motives we can't quite discern. In this ever-shifting world of global finance, where information, time, and money seem to move at faster and faster speeds, even smart, financially savvy investors can get a little dazed and confused.

I wrote this book to help you rise above the babble to become a more successful investor. If you're tired of being dazed and confused, susceptible to those who would profit at your expense, you can turn your experience right-side up and feel like the financial world is truly working for you.

To help you learn how to reap the rewards of the *investment markets*, previously available mainly to those selling investment products and advice—not you and me, this book starts with a history of markets tracing back to the dawn of civilization. You will see how markets and our understanding of them have changed. You will learn how the 1929 Wall Street Crash led to the construction of today's modern financial markets and how a deeper comprehension of investor behavior and investments since the Crash has led to exciting and profitable innovations.

You will learn how computers provided ways to test investment theories and how very smart people used computers to research and improve on established approaches to investing. Their early research led to the development of the first index fund. You will learn why index funds were a breakthrough in the investing world and how these same very smart people went on to develop more advanced funds that capture even higher returns! You will see that investors in these more advanced mutual funds have captured higher returns than the investors in index funds![1]

By the time you finish reading, I hope you will appreciate why I'm such a passionate advocate of the approaches I am detailing in these pages, and I hope you will understand how these approaches can help you change your life, the life of your family, and those who follow.

My Passion

Few things in life give peace of mind like knowing that you have a good doctor. I know that because my dad was a good doctor. Throughout my childhood, I watched closely as he practiced his craft—which was much more than medicine to him. His practice was about helping people, caring for the community, and providing a reliable service through the most vulnerable and difficult moments human beings can face.

As an orthopedist, he often gave care and comfort following a traumatic event. He was a true medical expert, yes, but he was much more. He understood that good healthcare was not just a matter of what you know, but also about understanding the person. It was about listening and treating people with humility and empathy.

One Saturday, I was with my dad as he visited his patients in the hospital. I watched from a distance as he met with a large man who was extremely agitated—almost dangerously so—about his injured son. Watching my dad respond to this man was a life-changing experience for me. Rather than back away, my dad gently touched the man, and I was amazed to see how quickly he calmed down. It was as if my dad had lifted the weight of the world off this man's shoulders. Watching my dad have that immediate impact on another human being made a lasting impression on me.

As you may have already guessed, my dad was my hero. In my own life, I have tried to walk in his footsteps. Indeed, I try to bring to my own work the same spirit of wisdom, humility, and service that animated my father's medical practice many years ago.

My choice of profession also came from watching my parents. As a teenager, I saw my mom and dad struggle with investing. Engaging stockbrokers recommended by wealthy patients provided disappointing results. When people would offer to "let them in" on investments, my dad would say, "if it's such a good deal, why are they offering it to me?" Watching them, I realized that I wanted to help people the way my father had, but with their financial health rather than physical health.

I had a lot to learn. In college, I majored in economics. In graduate school, I earned a master's in business administration with concentrations in finance and accounting. I then joined the international accounting firm, Coopers & Lybrand, and became a certified public accountant.

Building on what I learned in school and as a CPA, I joined Rosenberg Real Estate Equity Funds (RREEF) where I was quickly promoted to chief financial officer (CFO). There I saw how knowledgeable investors approached investing including their understanding of investments and investment markets. While at RREEF, I worked with my counterparts at the leading insurance companies and banks to form the National Council of Real Estate Investment Fiduciaries (NCREIF) and served as its first president and board chair. In this role, I gained firsthand knowledge of how professional investors throughout the U.S. approached investing, the information they required to support their investment decisions, and how they worked with their professional advisors.

Since my time at RREEF, I've worked as a technology entrepreneur and financial consultant in insurance, technology, real estate, equity markets, and more. My experience in financial markets is wide and varied. But I felt a growing sense that something was missing.

One day it struck me. I remembered what I really wanted to do. I wanted to follow in my dad's footsteps and focus on serving individuals and families. Instead of learning medicine to help others with their physical health, I could take my passion for finance and use the skills I learned as a CPA and CFO to help others with their financial health. Now I work as a financial advisor in the San Francisco Bay Area, and there is nothing I enjoy more than giving my clients the confidence that their futures and their legacies are in safe and secure hands.

Author's Note

This book is based on published reports of investment performance. Some are academic papers that have survived rigorous peer review. Others are studies of the performance of publicly traded mutual funds. As you probably know, individuals, their stockbrokers, and private money managers are not subject to the same regulatory controls as mutual funds; as a result, there are few studies of how well individuals do.

When most of us refer to mutual funds, we are usually referring to "open-end" funds. When investors buy or sell *shares* of an open-end fund, they do so directly with the fund's manager at a price based on the prices of all the securities owned by the fund at the end of the market's most recent trading session. The other type of mutual fund is a closed-end fund. Shares in a closed-end fund trade throughout the day like any other common stock on a stock exchange. Index funds are open-end mutual funds that are managed to track a market index. Electronically Traded Funds, or ETFs, are closed-end index funds with a few special features. More about these differences and when they matter later.

CHAPTER 1

THE MARKET

Markets have been a centerpiece of organized society since the dawn of civilization. Eight thousand years ago in the fertile plains of Mesopotamia, farming tools and new techniques allowed farmers to grow more food than they needed to survive. While most continued farming, some were able to shift to other work; to get excess crops into the hands of those who needed them, markets and exchanges developed.

Illustration 1–1. Image depicts beginning of ancient commerce. (Source: Shutterstock. Sokoto marketplace old view, Nigeria. Created by Hadamard after Barth, published on Le Tour du Monde, Paris, 1860)

As these exchanges grew and became more complex, currency was invented to facilitate trading. This process eventually led the way to what we now think of as investing—people entrusting their hard-earned savings to others in the hope that they will be paid more in return.

Investment Markets and Securities

Investing, as we know it, however, is a relatively new phenomenon. While markets and investment contracts date to the beginning of civilization, investing evolved into its modern form starting in the early nineteenth century.

Initially, investments were simply contracts called bills of exchange. They worked like our checks and were used by merchants to finance trade in the commodities they were buying and selling—grains, spices, silk, metals, and so on. Some merchants expanded beyond their own trading and formed merchant banks to invest in exchange-related instruments, profiting from financing long-distance trade. As they prospered, the merchant banks expanded their lending to monarchs, other royalty, and the papacy, usually gaining privileges, access, and side payments in return. Well-known examples include the Medici of Florence from the fourteenth and fifteenth centuries and the major British houses starting with the Barings in 1763 and Rothschilds later in the eighteenth century.

Eventually, some merchant banks entered the long-term capital financing business and began selling longer-term securities, including early versions of corporate stock, to nonfamily investors. By the nineteenth century, the growing credibility of governments, along with a larger investor base, permitted the extension of credit and the placement of government bonds with many investors.

Government debt securities dominated early investment offerings, particularly in times of war. Corporate investments took hold in places where the demand for long-term capital exceeded what was immediately available from an entrepreneur's personal network. The liberalization of incorporation rules aided this process. Indeed, modern-day investing requires the availability of corporate securities and of securities markets.

Such long-term corporate finance took many forms, including equity (a share of ownership) and debt instruments, which gave investors rights to a defined cash flow (or fixed income) without any ownership stake. Equity finance gave the shareholder some less-defined cash-flow rights and usually included some level of control rights—depending on how the corporate charter spelled out dividend payments to the various classes of shares.

Although debt securities held less profit potential than equity shares, they remained popular with outside investors who had little or no knowledge of a company and its management and also with owners (often families) who wanted to maintain control of their business. Equity shares, on the other hand, allowed risk sharing: founders and their heirs could divest part or all of their ownership and diversify their wealth, while outside investors seeking to profit could assume that risk.

During the early stages of investment markets there were few restrictions on the type of firm that could issue debt instruments but only certain types of corporations could issue equity shares. Many governments restricted incorporation through regulations and expensive legal hurdles, lengthy wait times, and high fees. This began to change during the industrial age when many countries removed such constraints in order to attract capital for economic expansion. The key feature of limited liability popularized these new equity securities because allowing entrepreneurs and investors to wall off their personal wealth from their business undertakings and investments lowered a major barrier to their investing in corporate equity.

The beginnings of the global railroad boom in the 1830s required significant long-term capital investment along with the need to manage the associated risk. The expansion of railroad networks brought advances in steel production and other large-scale industries. As the nineteenth century progressed, the need for capital from outside investors continued to expand.

This process of channeling funds from those with excess cash to those seeking it led to the development of our modern securities markets. Securities market *liquidity*—that is, ease and low cost of trading—reassured investors that they would be able to quickly sell their holdings in the future. Indeed, the most highly developed economies developed active securities markets. Interestingly, many early securities markets were built in the same locations where merchants had previously conducted their trades.

Investor Behavior

Although our modern investment markets emerged in order to fill a very important need for capital, some investors continue to think that the markets are just gambling pits where you place bets on winners and losers. Too often these attitudes lead to actions that are harmful to the investors' own financial health, although they may never understand that their mindset affects their investment success. Instead of thinking of investment markets as gambling pits, smart investors understand that markets are a "complex combination of miracles."[2]

Investment markets supply capital to enterprises that put it to productive use. This activity promotes the coordinated actions required by millions of people around the world to bring everything together. From this perspective, we see that *market prices* serve as a unifying force that enables millions of people to coordinate their actions efficiently.

Investment markets are also made up of millions of participants who voluntarily agree to buy and sell securities—stocks and bonds—based upon their own needs and strategies. Each day, millions of trades take place,[3] and the vast collective knowledge of all of these participants is pooled to set security prices.

This complex reality reveals the problems of the gambling-pit scenario. Investors who try to outguess the market are competing against the extraordinary collective wisdom of all of these buyers and sellers, including professional traders working for Wall Street investment banks, hedge funds, and computers armed with highly sophisticated trading programs. In effect, they are betting "against the house," and they often experience the same outcomes as gamblers at casinos. Most people who treat investment markets as a gambling pit end up with worse outcomes than they would experience if they trusted in "market forces." Professor Kenneth French has been quoted as saying, "The market is smarter than we are and no matter how smart we get, the market will always be smarter than we are."[4] In chapters to come, I will be telling you more about how to employ "market forces" to your benefit.

Market Turmoil

While markets usually operate effectively, there are times when they go astray, particularly as the hope of being paid more becomes contagious. Although only a relative few investors are affected most of the time, there have been occasions when the infection spreads and establishes itself as a dominant market force. This can happen when speculators note a fast increase in value of a given investment and decide to buy in anticipation of further increases, rather than because of the product's intrinsic value. The impact of speculation increases in size and influence when the news media jump on board and give it additional credibility. When something causes the speculators to lose their unrestrained enthusiasm, exuberance turns to disillusionment, which has sometimes led to panics that have weakened a nation's health and even its government. The rise and fall of speculative forces have become known as "bubbles." The first recorded speculative bubble was tulip mania.

Tulip Mania, The Netherlands (1636–1637)

In the seventeenth century, the Dutch Empire grew to become one of the major seafaring and economic powers. One outlet for its newfound wealth was an infatuation with the tulip, which had been imported in the late sixteenth century from the Ottoman Empire. At the peak of tulip mania, unrestrained exuberance became so irrational that speculators paid more than ten times the annual income of a skilled craftsman for the most highly valued tulip bulbs.

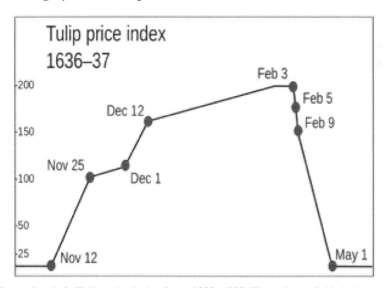

Illustration 1–2. Tulip price index from 1636–1637. The values of this index were compiled by Earl A. Thompson. (Source: Thompson, "The Tulipmania: Fact or Artifact?" *Public Choice* 130, nos. 1–2 (2007): 99–114, doi: 10.1007 / s11127–006 -9074–4)

The irrational exuberance did not last long. By February 1637, new buyers were no longer willing to pay increasingly inflated prices for their bulbs. As word spread, prices dropped and the speculative bubble burst. Fortunately, because the primary participants in tulip mania were wealthy merchants, the economic fallout from the bubble was limited.

South Sea Bubble, Great Britain (1720)

The South Sea Company was a British company founded in 1711. It was given its name to highlight the right to trade with South America as a way of distracting investors from its primary purpose, which was to consolidate and reduce the cost of national debt.

On several occasions the company offered to exchange government debt for stock. These offerings found limited success until 1719 when the House of Commons approved a new scheme for exchanging South Sea Company Stock for government debt. Shares backed by national debt were considered a safe investment. Well-connected politicians and others key to securing government favor were sold stock with options to sell the stock back to the company at any future date at the prevailing market price. This led to what became known as the Bubble Act, which gave a boost to the South Sea Company.

The price rose from £128 (pound sterling) in January 1720 to £1,000 in early August. When the company failed to pay dividends later in August, the price began to drop, falling faster than it had risen, to £150 by the end of September.

Many investors were ruined by the price collapse. The damage was so widespread that the British national economy was affected and the government was forced to introduce a series of measures to restore public confidence.

Great Wall Street Crash, United States (1929)

During most of the Roaring Twenties, the U.S. economy had been growing steadily. It was a technological golden age with innovations such as the radio, automobiles, airplanes, the telephone, and the power grid adding excitement to everyday living. Twenty million citizens took advantage of post-war prosperity and set out to make their fortunes in the stock market.

Some, no doubt, were influenced by Edgar Smith's *Common Stocks as Long Term Investments*, which was published in 1924. Prior to Smith, no data had been published on the market returns of long-term common stock investments in the U.S. market. The majority of investors did not invest in the common stock of industrial and commercial firms but instead focused on **bonds** or **preferred stock**. **Common stocks** were deemed "risky" and highly speculative.[5]

Smith's data showed the returns from common stocks had greatly exceeded the returns from corporate bonds. The total return on a portfolio of ten common stocks was 2.5 percent per year more than the total return on corporate bonds, when measured over sixty years. He suggested that investors could earn what modern finance theory calls an **equity risk premium** by holding ten common stocks over the long term, rather than corporate bonds.[6]

Furthering his theory, Smith introduced new ideas on the "riskiness" of stocks. He reported that "riskiness," which he defined as price volatility, was reduced:

- When the U.S. economy was more stable
- When investors held their stocks for four years or more
- When investors employed diversification—owning a broad variety of stocks to smooth out returns and reduce volatility

Companies that had pioneered many exciting innovations, like Radio Corporation of America (RCA) and General Motors, saw their stocks soar. Financial corporations also did well. Using the new findings, Wall Street bankers floated mutual fund companies (then known as "investment trusts") like the Goldman Sachs Trading Corporation. These investment trusts are known today as closed-end funds. Investment trusts pooled money and constructed diversified portfolios of common stocks that they then sold to the public as shares in the fund. While such an approach was capable of earning returns that substantially exceeded returns from bonds, most investors bought in after there had been a dramatic change in stock *valuations*, which were often far removed from the underlying *fundamental values*, a condition shared by previous market bubbles.

Infatuated by promises of "rags to riches" transformations and easy credit, many investors gave little thought to the risk that arose from widespread abuse of **leverage** through margin financing or unreliable information about the securities in which they were investing.

There was little support for federal regulation of the securities markets, and calls for the federal government to require financial disclosure and prevent the fraudulent sale of stock were never seriously pursued. And so the party continued.

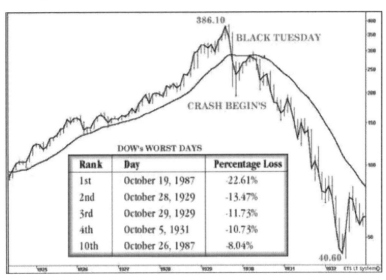

Illustration 1–3. Dow market crash after Black Tuesday.
(Source: Wikimedia Commons, by Mmakki)

When stock prices suddenly dropped in October 1929, public confidence in the markets also crashed. Many investors lost great sums of money in the collapse and struggled during the ensuing Great Depression. Economists and business and government leaders believed that the public's faith in the capital markets needed to be restored in order for the economy to recover.

Recent Turmoil

While the efforts to restore the public's faith in the capital markets went a long way toward addressing the worst abuses, they did not eliminate "irrational exuberance" that can still lead to dramatic swings in stock prices. Even after Congress passed laws in the 1930s and 1940s to regulate investment markets and investment advisers, the markets have seen significant turmoil, such as these two recent examples.

Dot-Com Bubble, Global Markets (1995–2001)

In the 1990s, the growing power and influence of personal computers began to overcome a major limitation: connectivity. The Internet, which had been developed to provide a common framework for military computers, provided a way over this barrier.

In the rush to take advantage of business to be gained from this growing connectivity, companies offered their services or end product for free with the expectation that they could build enough brand awareness to charge profitable rates for their services later. Armed with business plans that showed "hockey stick" shaped projections of rapid growth, venture capitalists chose to bring unproven investment concepts to market and let the market decide which would succeed.

The potential of these companies to transform lives and the economy caught the attention of Wall Street and the media. And the public was mesmerized by the promise of the potential. The "irrational exuberance" of the dot-com era came to a crashing halt when the business plans failed to deliver the cash needed to sustain the businesses.[7] As mounting evidence exposed the shortcomings of many of these business plans, exuberance turned to—you guessed it—disillusion.

Many investors who jumped on the dot-com bandwagon suffered greatly from the market collapse. Most unfortunate were those who had invested a large portion of their retirement savings in these dot-com companies.

Subprime Mortgage Crisis, Global Markets (2008)

As captured in the movie, *The Big Short,* a U.S. housing bubble burst in 2008. The main culprit was lackadaisical—some say fraudulent—oversight of mortgage lending. Because of compensation structures that rewarded mortgage companies for lending money with no penalty if the borrower failed to repay the debt, loan officers aggressively pursued lower-quality *subprime mortgages*.

Complicit with these lenders were the Wall Street firms who resold these loans as ***mortgage-backed securities*** and ***collateralized debt obligations (CDOs)*** and the ***ratings agencies*** that evaluated these financial products and gave them the very best ratings, despite their risks. While a few saw through the smoke screen being promoted by Wall Street, most disregarded the warning signs. And, as portrayed in the movie, even those who saw the coming collapse struggled to profit from their efforts to challenge market forces.

The eventual collapse of the housing bubble caused two of the most respected investment firms, Bear Stearns and Lehman Brothers, to shut their doors and led to a new law, the Dodd-Frank Wall Street Reform and Consumer Protection Act, enacted to help protect consumers from similar abuses in the future. Although stock market prices have recovered, many families have yet to recover the savings they lost in the collapse. Some speculate that many hurt by the 2008 collapse have rejected the politicians who were governing prior to and during the collapse. In Great Britain, this took the form of voting to leave the European Union—"Brexit." In the United States, some think this contributed to the election of Donald Trump as president.

Lessons Learned

Market forces are powerful. Over time their impact has expanded from the exclusive domain of royalty and wealthy merchants to anyone with savings to invest. And their power has grown from impacting a few to become a driving force behind world economic activity.

Market prices are the unifying force that enables millions of people to coordinate their actions efficiently but there are times when misguided sentiments dominate market forces, allowing speculation to drive prices far from historical norms. Fortunately, these times have been infrequent and tend not to last very long.

It should also be pointed out that during the twentieth century, investment scholars developed a more complete understanding of market prices and the forces that drive their movement. Significant advances have been made possible by increased computing power that was not available before 1960. Investment scholars and professionals believe that our more complete understanding of underlying market forces can be used to reduce the severity and disruption of future bubbles and market turmoil.

That said, it has been shown that investors who harness market forces, instead of reacting or trying to outguess them, reap more of the reward that investment markets have to offer.

In the next chapter you will learn how accounting standards, U.S. laws governing investors, investment brokers and advisers, investment markets, and the way information is communicated have evolved to give all investors an equal opportunity to profit.

CHAPTER 2

FOUNDATION FOR MODERN INVESTING

As mentioned in the previous chapter, investing began to evolve into its modern form in the nineteenth century, and it took a giant leap forward after the Wall Street Crash of 1929, which caused many investors to flee the market. The U.S. government and financial professionals took steps to restore the public's faith in the system so that they would return.

U.S. Investment Laws

Alarmed by the devastation caused by the Crash, the U.S. Senate established the Pecora Commission in 1932 to identify the causes and search for solutions. During the Commission's hearings, much of the blame for the Crash was attributed to groups of wealthy speculators who would conspire with the stock exchange specialists (floor traders charged with providing a market for the chosen stock) to drive up a stock's price.

Making matters worse, these speculators would use excessive amounts of borrowed money to buy more stock than they could personally afford to drive the stock's price up even further. They would then sell out, unloading the overpriced stocks on the unsuspecting public. Based on the findings in these hearings, Congress put in place the framework for today's investment markets through several important pieces of legislation.

The Securities Act of 1933

This law, together with the Securities Exchange Act of 1934, which created the *Securities and Exchange Commission (SEC)*, was designed to restore investor confidence in the U.S. capital markets by providing investors and the markets with more reliable information and clear rules of honest dealing. The main purpose of these laws can be reduced to two common-sense notions:

- Companies publicly offering securities for investment dollars must tell the public the truth about their businesses, the securities they are selling, and the risks involved in investing.
- People who sell and trade securities—brokers, dealers, and exchanges—must treat investors fairly and honestly.

Additionally, Congress prohibited fraudulent activities of any kind in connection with the offer, purchase, or sale of securities including insider trading, which is trading a security while in possession of relevant information that is not available to the general public.

Investment Company Act of 1940

This act regulates the organization of companies, including mutual funds, that engage primarily in investing, reinvesting, and trading in securities, and whose own securities are offered to the investing public. Designed to minimize conflicts of interest that arise in these complex operations, the act requires these companies to disclose their financial condition and investment policies to investors when stock is initially sold and on a regular basis thereafter. The act focuses on ensuring that the investing public receives information about the fund and its investment objectives, as well as about the investment company structure and operations.

Investment Advisers Act of 1940

This law regulates investment advisors and requires that firms or sole practitioners compensated for advising others about securities investments must register with the SEC and conform to regulations designed to protect investors. This law governs only "Registered Investment Advisors" or "RIAs". Registered representatives of security brokerage firms including investment banks and insurance companies are regulated by The Securities Exchange Act of 1934 ("Exchange Act").

Author's Note

As highlighted by the furor over the Fiduciary Rule proposed by the US Department of Labor in April 2016, there is a significant distinction between regulations governing RIA's and the regulations governing security brokerage firms and their representatives. RIA's are required to avoid conflicts of interest and commit in writing to put their clients' interests first, which is known as serving as a *fiduciary*. Brokerage firms are governed by a "suitability" standard, which means the financial products are suitable to the customer. When presented with a "suitable" investment, investors need to remember the old saying, "buyer beware," and carefully consider whether what is "suitable" is in their best interest.

Financial Professionals

Financial professionals also took steps after the Crash to restore the public's faith in the capital markets. The accounting profession formalized rules to improve the reliability of information that investors were using to make their buying and selling decisions. Investment professionals published techniques for pricing securities. Financial statisticians provided guidance on what investors could expect in the way of *investment returns* through the development of market indexes. (More on indexes later).

Accounting

While the early development of accounting dates back to ancient Mesopotamia, it began to transition into an organized profession in the nineteenth century, with local professional bodies in England merging to form the Institute of Chartered Accountants in England and Wales in

1880. In the United States, the American Institute of Accountants was established in 1887.

Following the Wall Street Crash, the American Institute of Accountants (now known as the American Institute of Certified Public Accountants) set up a committee to establish accounting standards to rationalize and legitimize the reporting of business performance. These accounting standards, and those that followed, enhanced the reliability of the data needed by investors to make informed investment decisions.

Since the 1930s, accounting standards have expanded in breadth and depth of the issues addressed. U.S. accounting standards are now established by the Financial Accounting Standards Board (FASB) and the SEC, which coordinate with their international counterparts to promote consistency across all investment markets.

New Ideas About How to Value Common Stock

It should come as no surprise that after the market crashed in 1929, there was a movement away from Smith's valuation theory. Benjamin Graham, David Dodd, and John Burr Williams analyzed the Smith valuation method and introduced new and more reliable ideas about how to value common stocks.

In 1934, Graham and Dodd of Columbia Business School published *Security Analysis,* in which they encouraged investors to take an entirely different approach.[8] They focused on corporate earnings and book value. And they selected stocks that were trading below their tangible book value as a safeguard to adverse future developments that could be encountered in the stock market.

In 1938, John Burr Williams published *The Theory of Investment Value.*[9] Similar to Graham and Dodd, he focused on an investment's intrinsic value, shifting the focus away from Smith's interpretation of historical performance to the underlying method for calculating an investment's value.

Williams proposed what has become the standard concept used to price securities: that the value of an asset should be the present value of its future net cash flows that an investor expects to receive from dividend distributions and interest payments and an eventual selling price, or return of principal. But what does this mean?

Present value is actually a simple concept. It comes from the time-value of money, which is the idea that individuals do not like to wait. Just walk through a toy store with a young child. Watch as a child's joy over a shiny new toy turns into a tantrum when told no, he cannot have that toy today. Even though we may grow older and, hopefully, more mature, there's still a young child inside us wanting to have it NOW! What we can have sooner is worth more to us than what we have to wait for.

The brilliance of these ideas should not be understated. They continue to provide the foundation for valuing securities and enable investors to shift their focus to how to profit from this foundation.

Market Indexes

Although standardized financial reporting and quantitative approaches to value stocks and bonds helped investors choose more wisely, additional information was needed to restore their faith in the investment markets. Investors wanted to know how they were faring compared to other investors and to the overall market. This led to the development of investment market indexes, which track the changes in the value of investments over time.

Indexes work like a summary of the market by tracking the price changes of a group of investments within a market segment or the entire market. Investors can use indexes to compare the performance of their investments to a market segment such as tech stocks or British stocks or to all stocks. Indexes have become so widely adopted that when people talk about the market going up or down, showing a strong performance or a weak one, or turning bull or bear, they are almost always referring to the market as seen through the lens of indexes.

Beginning with the Dow

The first indexes were actually developed before the market crashed in 1929 but not widely used at the time. When Charles H. Dow, a finance journalist, unveiled the first stock index in 1896, most adults had spent their childhoods in mines, factories, and fields rather than schools.

Their idea of a market was a place with stalls where you could browse farmers' produce and buy your groceries. The idea of buying the performance—or profit—of a company was a difficult concept to grasp.

Making matters worse were loose regulations of the day. Published information wasn't guaranteed to be accurate or even truthful. There was nothing to stem the fraud flowing from the unscrupulous brokers and dealers who circled around Wall Street, waiting for investors they could exploit.

To overcome the lack of reliable information and to help investors gain more confidence, Mr. Dow created the Dow Jones Industrial Average (DJIA). He initially decided it should be an average of the prices of the top twelve stocks in the market and considered his average as a measure of the market's tide. Armed with this measure, Dow was able to see whether the market rose for a consecutive period, as with a bull market, or if it regularly fell, as with a bear market.

In 1928, it became necessary to switch the method of calculating the Dow indexes because companies that comprised the Dow were involved in mergers and stock splits that warped the numbers. The Dow Jones Industrial Average is still around today, using the method revised by Charles Dow in 1928.

S&P 500

Standard Statistics Bureau began tracking ninety stocks in 1926.[10] One characteristic distinguishing this index from the more popular Dow Jones Industrial Average was that it was a market-weighted average that took into account the market value of each company. Although this meant that bigger companies had a greater impact on the index value, they didn't sway the ninety as much as the highest-priced stocks in the Dow affected the DJIA calculation. However, this more accurate measure of the overall market was not as widely followed as the Dow Jones until much later.

In 1941, Standard Statistics merged with the company that Henry Varnum Poor had founded in 1860 to provide a financial history of all the companies laying track or digging canals in the United States to form Standard and Poor's. In 1957, Standard & Poor's expanded its index to 500 companies; most of us now call this index "the S&P 500."

NASDAQ
In 1971, the National Association of Securities Dealers (NASD) introduced the world's first electronic stock exchange: NASDAQ. The AQ stands for automated quotations. Over time it handled the majority of trades formerly executed by the "over-the-counter" (OTC) system of trading. OTC refers to stocks that trade via a network of securities dealers who agree to buy and sell these stocks instead of using a centralized market or *exchange*. Initially, the NASDAQ attracted new *growth companies*, such as Apple, Microsoft, CISCO and Oracle.

In 1985, NASDAQ introduced its own index, the NASDAQ Composite, to compete with the S&P. The NASDAQ Composite Index was designed as a market-weighted index that contained many companies from the technology *sector*—largely unmapped territory at the time.

Now, thanks to the power of computing, there are many market-tracking tools and indexes in addition to the Dow, the S&P, and the NASDAQ. In fact, it should be noted that advances in our knowledge of market forces has been driven since the 1960's largely by advances in computing power.

Lessons Learned
The laws passed after the Crash, the new, unified accounting rules, new stock valuation techniques, and the development of new indexes restored the public's faith in the capital markets and laid the foundation for the effective functioning of modern capital markets. As you will read in the next chapter, these advances led to the next leap in our understanding of investment markets and investing.

CHAPTER 3

INTRODUCTION OF SECURITY SELECTION

Armed with the ideas presented by Graham and Dodd and John Burr Williams, investors set out to find a good stock and buy it at the best price. One investor, Gerald Loeb, a founding partner of E. F Hutton & Co., championed the idea of "superior investment performance." In *The Battle for Investment Survival,* originally published in 1935, Loeb captured the prevailing view that "Once you attain competency, diversification is undesirable. One or two, or at most three or four, securities should be bought. Competent investors will never be satisfied beating the averages by a few small percentage points."[11]

Many embraced Loeb's message, viewing investment markets as a competitive playing field and believing all an investor had to do to be successful was to work harder and smarter than amateurs and bureaucrats did. Do you remember the television ad, "When E. F. Hutton talks, people listen?" Maybe it was referring to Loeb.

Early on, Loeb seemed credible. Institutions were involved in less than 10 percent of the daily trades on the *New York Stock Exchange* while individuals were involved in more than 90 percent. Insurance companies and bank trust departments dominated institutional investing. They were conservative and hierarchical, controlled by investment committees of senior executives who were risk averse. These investors preferred investments that paid *dividends* and interest rather than those whose price was expected to rise. When they bought bonds, they avoided the risk of changing market values by buying high-grade bonds in *laddered maturities*. Trading securities was considered "highly speculative."

During this time, most individual investors were amateurs without access to meaningful research who made their decisions on what to buy or sell sporadically, buying when they received money, such as an inheritance or a bonus, and selling to pay for college tuition or make a down payment on a home. Brokerage houses controlled the buying and selling of stocks and the information provided to their clients. Individual investors were satisfied with a modest profit and had few tools to measure their performance beyond what the brokerage houses told them.

The competitive landscape began to change after World War II when many talented young investment professionals entered the competition seeking market-beating performance. They listened to Gerald Loeb and were confident that because they were hard-working, well-informed, boldly active professionals, they not only *could* beat the competition, but they *would*.

Growth of Professional Money Management

Loeb was not alone in his belief that competent investors could be expected to beat the market averages. Mutual fund companies, some of which dated back to the closed-end funds that contributed to the Great Wall Street Crash, promoted the same ideas.

Corporate pension assets were accumulating rapidly in postwar America. New investment firms were organized to compete for the pension business. Their main promise: we have the most talented young analysts and portfolio managers who will be first to find and act on investment opportunities that would meet or beat the results of the mutual funds. Aided by *Bloomberg machines*, algorithms, and an array of other new tools for gathering and analyzing data, many of these managers were very successful. RREEF's sister firm, Rosenberg Capital Management, was a shining example of a firm formed to pursue the demand for superior performance.[12]

A. G. Becker and Merrill Lynch created a new service to measure each pension fund's investment performance against that of competitors, demonstrating that the banks' investment performance was often disappointing compared with that of the new firms. The pension funds began pulling their money out of bank trust departments and pouring it into the new investment firms that promised superior performance. After Fidelity and other mutual fund companies reported earning superior rates of return in the 1960s, mutual fund sales boomed.

Investing 1.0

Illustration 3–1. 20hp Minerva chassis, side elevation (Source: Wikimedia Commons)

Similar to an auto built on a 1930s chassis, the investment approach employed by these professional money managers was built on 1930s investment theories. Firms would establish their expertise in an industry or sector or type of company. As depicted in illustration 3–2, these firms would buy a handful of securities expected to do well in the future and sell securities expected to not do well. Before computers and online access to company data, the number of investments these firms could manage was limited by the size of their staff.

Taking a cue from Silicon Valley where software is updated from time to time and initial versions are often labeled version 1.0, we can describe this approach developed in the 1930s as "Investing 1.0." Because it focuses only on pricing individual securities, it can also be described as one-dimensional.

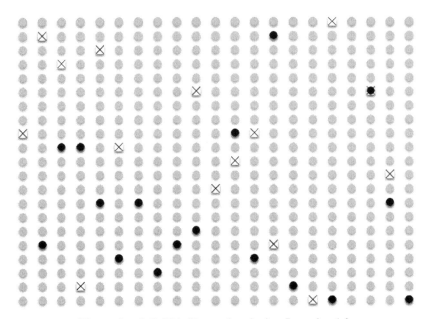

Illustration 3–2. This illustration depicts Investing 1.0.

In this illustration, each dot represents an investment security. The black dots are individual securities that the investment manager wants to buy, believing they will outperform the others in the market. The "X"'s are individual securities to sell because they are believed to be overvalued; if owned, they are expected to underperform the market. As you can see in this illustration, determining which handful of securities will outperform the market is like finding a needle in a haystack.

Note that this type of manager starts with nothing and finds a reason, or is given a reason, to pick one security over another. Often the reason is the manager's belief that a specific security is overpriced or underpriced. But this investment approach of choosing only a few stocks often results in inadequate diversification and higher risk. Equally important, the manager's frequent buying and selling results in high costs to the investor. In essence, Investing 1.0 is based on predicting and forecasting the future. In addition to investment firms that tout their skill for picking securities that will perform well, other firms tout their ability to predict the future direction of the economy or the stock market itself (*aka* market timing). Echoing ideas promoted by the media, they will say things like, "We have a proven system for picking winning stocks," or "That sector will continue advancing through next year," or "The market is primed for a retreat."

Investing 1.0 assumes that someone has a crystal ball.

"How do the year end numbers look?"

Illustration 3–3. (Source: Shutterstock, **Stock illustration ID: 245692315**)

Unfortunately for those who continue to employ this approach, times have changed. Today, the competitive landscape of eighty years ago has changed, and the advantages touted by professional money managers too often fail to deliver the promised results. More than 95 percent of trades in listed stocks, and nearly 100 percent of other security transactions, are executed by full-time professionals who are constantly comparison-shopping inside the market for any competitive advantage.

Performance of Investing 1.0

Armed with research and a continuous flood of global market information, economic analyses, industry studies, risk metrics, company reports, and sophisticated computer-driven analytical models, investment professionals now have access to more market information than they can possibly use. With competition at such a high level, it is understandable that few are sufficiently more hard-working, more highly disciplined, or more creative than their counterparts.

After eighty years of compounding changes in investment management and in the security markets, few fund managers beat the market. Only a small fraction of those who succeed in beating the market are able to continue to do so. One of the dark secrets of modern investing involves performance rankings of fund managers, which has become increasingly meaningless. Despite the claims individuals and firms make to tout their ability to beat the market, independent research has found that superior performance using Investing 1.0 is primarily a function of luck.[13]

Note: Mutual funds are the only investment portfolios that publicly report performance daily; so, the following information about performance is based on data provided by the mutual funds. Most mutual funds managed by professionals who use Investing 1.0 fail to outperform—or "beat"—their benchmarks, and the percentage of funds that outperform their benchmarks declines as the years measured increases.

Some investors try to improve these odds by picking managers whose funds have outperformed their benchmarks in the past. Unfortunately, using past track records has proven to be futile because most fund managers who *do* deliver superior performance for a period of time rarely continue to do so.

Of U.S. domiciled equity mutual funds, only a third of recent "winners" (funds that beat their benchmarks) continue to do so. A longer history of market-beating performance does not lead to better results. While the percentages may vary from time to time, the evidence shows that those managers using Investing 1.0 cannot be relied on to live up to their promise of beating the market over the long haul. Similar results were found for U.S. domiciled fixed income mutual funds.

Results similar to those measured with mutual funds have been found in sovereign wealth funds[14] and private foundations[15] as well when their investment managers use Investing 1.0.

Manager underperformance is not necessarily due to a lack of knowledge or expertise. In fact, the professional investment managers I know are very bright, knowledgeable, and hard-working. But this high level of expertise and motivation results in intense market competition, which drives prices to fair value.

Benjamin Graham, whose theory on value helped launch Investing 1.0, recognized the difficulty when interviewed in 1976:

Most of the stockbrokers, financial analysts, investment advisers, etc., are above average in intelligence, business honesty and sincerity. But . . . They tend to take the market and themselves too seriously. They spend a large part of their time trying, valiantly and ineffectively, to do things they can't do well. . . . To forecast short- and long-term changes in the economy, and in the price level of common stocks, to select the most promising industry groups and individual issues—generally for the near-term future.[16]

Peter Lynch, the legendary manager of Fidelity's Magellan Fund, reinforced this view when he said, "All the time and effort that people devote to picking the right fund, the hot hand, the great manager, have in most cases led to no advantage."[17]

While some characterize this as a sign of the market being efficient, I view it as a sign that the competition is ruthless. If someone finds a way to achieve higher returns, others will quickly adopt the technique and the gap will narrow until the method no longer provides a competitive advantage.

Lessons Learned

Investing 1.0 has enriched Wall Street and fuels the financial media. But you have seen in this chapter that many investors and investment professionals using this approach fail to deliver the market-beating performance they expect and you have been promised. In the following chapter, you'll learn why this approach falls short.

CHAPTER 4

THE PROBLEM

W hy do very capable people using Investing 1.0 often fail to beat the market? Why do the investments they select typically return less than what an investor would make by simply capturing the average for the entire stock market? These less-than stellar results often occur because it is enormously difficult to achieve all four conditions that are needed to ensure superior market-beating performance. Examining those four conditions will allow us to understand the role they play in market performance and to understand why it is so difficult to consistently align all these elements using Investing 1.0.

Four Conditions

As we saw in the last chapter, the individual securities selection approach to investing involves *forecasting*. Although many professionals (along with friends and neighbors) present their forecasts with great confidence, investors are unlikely to profit from them because using forecasting to beat the market requires four elements:

1. Other investors cannot yet know or understand what is behind your forecast.
2. Your forecast must be accurate and there must be sufficient history of reliable forecasts for you to trust them enough to take action.

3. When others learn what you know, they must react the way that you expect, causing the market to move in the way you want it to move.

4. The value gained by the market movement must exceed the costs you incurred in gathering the information to make the forecast and in buying and selling the securities involved.

Let's examine these four conditions in more detail to understand the roles they play.

Condition 1: Early Knowledge

Early knowledge is a term I use for knowing something that other investors do not yet know or understand.

It is a daunting task, and a much greater challenge than just outwitting you or me or the dummy next door. Early knowledge involves competing with the collective knowledge of all investors. You need to be smarter than all other investors, including the rocket scientists working for hedge funds and Wall Street firms. The competition is so fierce, even among the most successful firms, that no one has developed a persistent competitive advantage.

Pundits in the media and authoritative investment publications don't help. When they make their predictions, they usually cite experts who shared their insights. This means that you are getting the story at the same time as many, perhaps millions, of others and after experts who may have already acted on the information.

What about getting the inside scoop on your own? The laws passed following the Great Wall Street Crash of 1929 prohibited trading a security based on information not shared with all investors. The rules and regulations and the ability of regulatory agencies to prosecute those who violate the rules have led to a more level playing field in the investment markets. If you look at the recent convictions of some prominent hedge fund managers, you know that getting and using insider information is not a good idea.

Those laws also ensure that prices of individual securities already reflect the effects of available information—"events that have already occurred and events which investors expect to take place in the future." [18] This concept is referred to as market efficiency.

To illustrate the concept of investment market efficiency, think about the process of buying or selling a home. You hire a realtor who knows your local market and can make others aware that your house is for sale. One of the first things a good realtor will do is advise you on what selling price you should expect and what strategies to employ for getting that price. Among the strategies is getting word out to all potential buyers, generally by telling other realtors, especially those representing buyers looking to buy a house in your area. However, even with those efforts and despite the development of online listing services, you are not certain that all potential buyers know about your house and you are never quite sure whether the price you are seeking is too high or too low. In other words, the real estate market is not very efficient.

Contrast this experience with buying and selling publicly traded securities. There are many sites where you can see the price of the last trade of each security listed in the market. Prices change quickly to adjust to new information, such as earnings announcements and the most recent trades. When unexpected events occur or investors change their expectations for whatever reason, security prices adjust at lightning speed. Computers monitoring news sources throughout the world are programmed to immediately buy or sell based on the new information. This process exemplifies what we mean by the term "efficient market."

Illustration 4–1 shows how quickly the market responded to the news that Berkshire Hathaway was acquiring the H. J. Heinz Company.

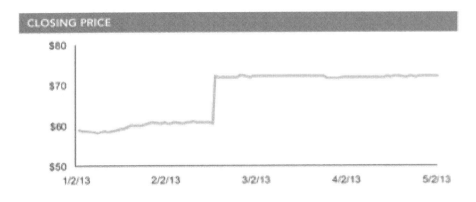

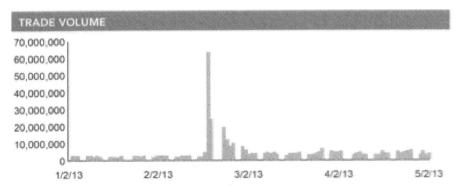

Illustration 4–1. Price and trading volume of H. J. Heinz Company stock reacted quickly to news that Berkshire Hathaway was acquiring the H. J. Heinz Company.

You can see that the price moved and trading activity peaked almost instantly when the announcement was made. A more recent example occurred on December 6, 2016, when Boeing's stock price changed within twenty seconds of Donald Trump's unexpected tweet about Boeing's contract for a new Air Force One plane. Because the market incorporates new information so quickly, it is simply unrealistic for the average investor to think he or she can profit from acting before others learn and respond to new information.

To get ahead of this market efficiency without violating the insider trading laws, you need to do your own detective work. An example is field research that was conducted by my colleagues at Rosenberg Capital

Management (RCM). Along with other activities, they would employ researchers to count cars in parking lots of shopping centers. Despite all their talent and resources, RCM was unable to convert their knowledge into a persistent competitive advantage.

In his finance book, *A Random Walk Down Wall Street*, Burton Malkiel explained why Nobel laureates and other leading economists believe profiting from mispriced securities is so difficult. "Many of us economists who believe in efficiency do so because we view markets as amazingly successful devices for reflecting new information rapidly and, for the most part, accurately."[19] Nobel laureate Merton Miller observed, "Everybody has some information. The function of the markets is to aggregate that information, evaluate it, and get it incorporated into prices."[20]

Condition 2: Accurate Forecast

To make an accurate forecast, someone needs special insight enabling him or her to better predict the path that prices will follow. As you will see in chapter 6, scientific study of the stock market's performance has identified predictable investment patterns. However, the time frames involved in such studies are long-term. The studies found too much "noise"—day-to-day variability—to identify patterns that would lend themselves to the types of forecasts used in Investing 1.0.

In Illustration 4–2, I use annual returns to illustrate how difficult it is to find meaningful information to make an accurate forecast while using Investing 1.0. Investment patterns relying on shorter time periods, such as monthly, weekly, or daily results, are even less likely to provide information that leads to profitable investment decisions.

In the chart of annual returns in the U.S. stock market from 1926 through 2015, the circles represent the annual returns of the entire market. The black squares represent the annual returns of small cap stocks trading on the U.S. stock market. There is no predictable pattern for either the entire market or for the higher-returning, but more volatile, small cap stocks.

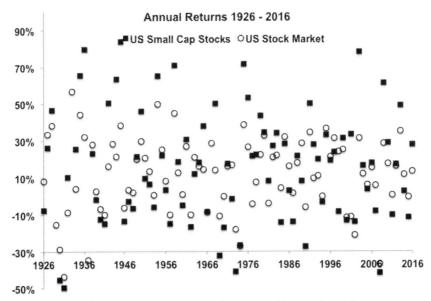

Illustration 4–2. Annual returns of the entire U.S. stock market are displayed in white circles with black lines; annual returns of small cap stocks are displayed in black squares. (Source: Graph developed from CRSP Deciles 1–10 Index [market] vs CRSP Deciles 9–10 Index)

Illustration 4–3 displays the global picture of developed countries from 1997 through 2016. If the numbers were large enough to read, you would see how the rankings of annual returns of each country's stock market change every year—with no predictable pattern. The highlighted squares identify the country with the highest annual return for that year.

	1997	1998	1999	2000	2001	2002	2003	2004	2005	2006	2007	2008	2009	2010	2011	2012	2013	2014	2015	2016
Australia	-10.4	6.1	17.6	-10.0	1.7	-1.3	49.5	30.3	16.0	30.9	28.3	-50.7	76.4	14.5	-11.0	22.1	4.2	-3.4	-10.0	11.4
Austria	1.6	0.4	-9.1	-12.0	-5.6	16.5	57.0	71.5	24.6	36.5	2.2	-68.4	43.2	9.9	-36.4	25.9	13.4	-29.8	3.5	11.3
Belgium	13.6	67.7	-14.3	-16.8	-10.9	-15.0	36.3	43.5	9.0	36.7	-2.7	-66.5	57.5	-0.4	-10.6	39.6	27.6	4.1	12.1	-7.6
Canada	12.8	-6.1	53.7	5.3	-20.4	-13.2	54.6	22.2	28.3	17.8	29.6	-45.5	56.2	20.5	-12.7	9.1	5.6	1.5	-24.2	24.6
Denmark	34.5	9.0	12.1	3.4	-14.8	-16.0	49.3	30.8	24.5	38.8	25.8	-47.6	36.6	30.7	-16.0	31.3	25.2	6.2	23.4	-15.8
Finland	17.3	121.6	152.6	-14.2	-38.2	-30.3	19.4	6.1	16.7	29.9	48.7	-55.2	11.1	10.3	-31.9	14.6	48.0	-0.7	2.0	-4.7
France	11.9	41.5	29.3	-4.3	-22.4	-21.2	40.2	18.5	9.9	34.5	13.2	-43.3	31.8	-4.1	-16.9	21.3	26.3	-9.9	-0.1	4.9
Germany	24.6	29.4	20.0	-15.6	-22.4	-33.2	63.8	16.2	9.9	36.0	35.2	-45.9	25.2	8.4	-18.1	30.9	31.4	-10.4	-1.9	2.8
Hong Kong	-23.3	-2.9	59.5	-14.7	-18.6	-17.8	38.1	25.0	8.4	30.4	41.2	-51.2	60.2	23.2	-16.0	28.3	11.1	5.1	-0.5	2.3
Ireland	15.8	35.3	-12.6	-12.7	-2.8	-26.2	43.8	43.1	-2.3	46.8	-20.1	-71.9	12.3	-18.1	13.7	5.7	41.2	2.3	16.5	-7.1
Italy	35.5	52.5	-0.3	-1.3	-26.6	-7.3	37.8	32.5	1.9	32.5	6.1	-50.0	26.6	-15.0	-23.2	12.5	20.4	-9.5	2.3	-10.5
Japan	-23.7	5.1	61.5	-28.2	-29.4	-10.3	35.9	15.9	25.5	6.2	-4.2	-29.2	6.3	15.4	-14.3	8.2	27.2	-4.0	9.6	2.4
Netherlands	23.8	23.2	6.9	-4.1	-22.1	-20.8	28.1	12.2	13.9	31.4	20.6	-48.2	42.3	1.7	-12.1	20.6	31.3	-3.5	1.3	4.8
New Zealand	-14.1	-22.6	12.9	-33.5	8.4	24.2	55.4	35.2	1.7	16.6	8.9	-53.8	50.4	8.3	5.5	29.3	11.3	7.3	-6.3	18.4
Norway	6.2	-30.1	31.7	-0.9	-12.2	-7.3	48.1	53.3	24.3	45.1	31.4	-64.2	87.1	10.9	-10.0	18.7	9.4	-22.0	-15.0	13.3
Singapore	-30.0	-12.9	99.4	-27.7	-23.4	-11.0	37.6	22.3	14.4	46.7	28.4	-47.4	74.0	22.1	-17.9	31.0	1.7	3.0	-17.7	1.4
Spain	25.4	49.9	4.8	-15.9	-11.4	-15.3	58.5	28.9	4.4	49.4	24.0	-40.6	43.5	-22.0	-12.3	3.0	31.3	4.7	-15.6	-1.0
Sweden	12.9	14.0	79.7	-21.3	-27.2	-30.5	64.5	36.3	10.3	43.4	0.6	-49.9	64.2	33.8	-16.0	22.0	24.5	-7.5	-5.0	0.6
Switzerland	44.2	23.5	-7.0	6.9	-21.4	-10.3	34.1	15.0	16.3	27.4	5.3	-30.5	25.3	11.8	-6.8	20.4	26.6	-0.1	0.4	-4.9
UK	22.6	17.8	12.5	-11.5	-14.0	-15.2	32.1	19.6	7.4	30.6	8.4	-48.3	43.3	8.8	-2.6	15.3	20.7	-5.4	-7.6	-0.1
US	33.4	30.1	21.9	-12.8	-12.4	-23.1	28.4	10.1	5.1	14.7	5.4	-37.6	26.3	14.8	1.4	15.3	31.8	12.7	0.7	10.9

Illustration 4–3. Annual returns of developed countries arranged from highest to lowest. (Source: Dimensional Fund Advisors, Master Slide Library Published March 25, 2017, PowerPoint Slide Number 65)

Both illustrations (4.2 and 4.3) highlight the futility of using Investing 1.0 to try to forecast stock market behavior in short time horizons.

Condition 3: Others' Reactions

Even if you get information ahead of everyone else and make an accurate forecast, you won't profit unless the market responds as you predict. You want to buy securities before prices go up and sell securities before prices go down.

An example is when pundits predict the US Federal Reserve will change the interest rates it charges banks. The predictions are usually accompanied by insights into "leading economic indicators". If the economy or job growth is too weak, the Fed is expected to lower interest rates. If too strong or there is concern about rising inflation, the Fed is expected to raise interest rates. Because banks pass on these interest rate changes, these changes are expected to affect stock prices. Rising interest rates lower corporate profits, which are expected to cause stock prices to go down. Lowering interest rates is expected to increase corporate profits and stock prices.

As we have recently seen, even when pundits forecast correctly and the Fed changes rates as expected, there are times when stock prices don't respond as predicted. Just look at the rise in stock prices after the Fed raised interest rates from 1.0% to 1.25% on June 14, 2017.

As you can see, there are several conditions that must be met for you to profit from short-term forecasts: early knowledge, accurate forecasting and others following as expected. So, the next time you hear pundits talking about the Fed, see if the stock market reacts as they predict.

Condition 4: Cost-Effective Value

Even when the first three conditions are met, you still have to clear one more barrier before profiting from short-term forecasts: your performance will need to beat the market by more than what it costs to find the investment opportunities and execute the strategy. To develop a competitive advantage over major investment firms, you need to hire your own "rocket scientists," employ big computers and databases, and hire global research teams and other resources. As you might imagine, this process will be expensive—very expensive. To be profitable, you will need to reduce your average cost by spreading it over a large pool of investment dollars, and your performance will need to beat the market by more than what it costs to find the investment opportunities and execute the strategy.

Nobel Laureate Eugene Fama and Ken French explored this idea and found that funds using Investing 1.0 to invest in U.S. equities effectively performed the same as the market of U.S. equities—before expenses. The performance was lower than the market by the amount of the expenses.[21]

The illustration 4–4 shows how these expenses affect the performance of mutual funds. These U.S. equity mutual funds are grouped by expense ratios. (The groupings are by "quartile." Low includes funds whose expense ratio is in the bottom 25%, i.e. less than 75%

of mutual funds. Medium low includes funds whose expense ratio is more than the bottom 25% and less than the top 50%. Medium high expense ratios are more than the bottom 50% and less than the top 25%. High are the funds with expense ratios among the highest 25%.). Each fund is compared to its respective benchmark. The percentage of funds beating their benchmarks declines as the average expense ratio increases.

	Low	Medium Low	Medium High	High
From January 1, 2011 through December 31, 2015				
% Above Benchmark	40%	33%	30%	21%
% Below Benchmark	**60%**	**67%**	**70%**	**79%**
Average Expense Ratio	*0.71%*	*1.06%*	*1.27%*	*1.67%*
From January 1, 2006 through December 31, 2015				
% Above Benchmark	30%	24%	18%	11%
% Below Benchmark	**70%**	**76%**	**82%**	**89%**
Average Expense Ratio	*0.75%*	*1.12%*	*1.36%*	*1.83%*
From January 1, 2001 through December 31, 2015				
% Above Benchmark	26%	20%	15%	7%
% Below Benchmark	**74%**	**80%**	**85%**	**93%**
Average Expense Ratio	*0.83%*	*1.21%*	*1.49%*	*2.05%*

Illustration 4–4. Performance of U.S. equity mutual funds compared by expense ratios. (Source: Dimensional Fund Advisors, Master Slide Library Published March 25, 2017, PowerPoint Slide Number 90)

Another type of expense, which is more difficult to measure and is often overlooked in considering fund expenses, is turnover—the cost associated with buying and selling securities. When you buy or sell a security, you pay both a commission and what is known as the *bid / ask spread.* For mutual funds that are motivated to move quickly, buying or selling large blocks of securities often proves to be very costly.

Illustration 4–5 shows how turnover expenses affect the performance of mutual funds. These U.S. equity mutual funds are grouped by quartile of turnover percentage and compared to their respective benchmarks. Winners reported higher returns than their benchmarks. Losers reported lower returns than their benchmarks.

	Low	Medium Low	Medium High	High
From January 1, 2011 through December 31, 2015				
% Above Benchmark	36%	33%	29%	26%
% Below Benchmark	**64%**	**67%**	**71%**	**74%**
Average Turnover	*20%*	*46%*	*75%*	*169%*
From January 1, 2006 through December 31, 2015				
% Above Benchmark	31%	23%	15%	14%
% Below Benchmark	**69%**	**77%**	**85%**	**86%**
Average Turnover	*24%*	*53%*	*84%*	*180%*
From January 1, 2001 through December 31, 2015				
% Above Benchmark	29%	19%	12%	8%
% Below Benchmark	**71%**	**81%**	**88%**	**92%**
Average Turnover	*28%*	*61%*	*94%*	*215%*

Illustration 4–5. Performance of U.S. equity mutual funds compared by turnover percentages. (Source: Dimensional Fund Advisors, Master Slide Library Published March 25, 2017, PowerPoint Slide Number 92)

As you can see, investors find it difficult to meet each of the four conditions involved in beating the market. No wonder so few professional investors do. But, even this doesn't tell the whole story, as other factors also contribute to the success or failure rate of investors using Investing 1.0.

Bad Behavior

Illustration 4–6. (Source: Flickr. Walt Kelly's "Pogo")

The chief problem of Investing 1.0 is that it reflects how we're wired to think. Unfortunately, we human beings are not wired for investing.

From groundbreaking research in behavioral finance that began in the 1970s, we have learned that our natural instincts lead to a chain of mental errors that result in faulty reasoning for investing. Illustration 4–7 displays some of the typical mental errors that affect our decision-making processes when investing.

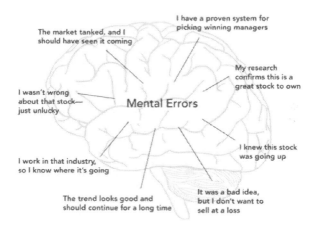

Illustration 4–7. Mental errors that can affect investment decisions.

The most common errors occur in the "emotional curve of investing" as displayed in Illustration 4–8. By reacting to market activity, we fall prey to our emotions, buying when feeling elated and selling when scared.

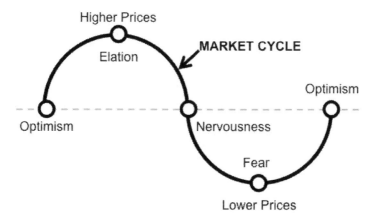

Illustration 4–8. The emotional curve of investing can wreak havoc on performance.

The media know about this phenomenon and can stoke fears or elation by their reporting and particularly through the use of dramatic headlines, such as "The Death of Equities"[22] or "The Crash of '98, Can the US Economy Hold Up?"[23] or "How to Reach $1 Million."[24]

Wall Street firms also know about these common mental errors and emotional curves, and they use them to their advantage when promoting their expertise to potential clients. Falling prey to emotions affects investment performance, and no one—no matter how sophisticated—is immune to it.

Individual Investors Earn Less

Individual investors often earn less than the returns reported by the mutual funds they invest in, in part, because of the impact of taxes. Because mutual funds pass the responsibility for paying taxes on income and capital gains to their investors, mutual funds report their performance before income taxes. Investors' returns are calculated after taxes.

Another reason individual investors earn less is related to the Morningstar effect. A variation on the emotional curve, the Morningstar effect describes how investors use Morningstar's ratings to chase investment performance. Although Morningstar publishes mutual fund ratings primarily based on their past performance, individual investors too often interpret these ratings to mean the fund manager has a special skill for selecting securities, which makes them want in on the future action. They jump on board and pour money into mutual funds with a four- or five-star rating or they sell their *shares* in a fund that receives a one- or two-star rating. Unfortunately, too often, the performance that earned a fund a four- or five-star rating does not continue after monies start flowing into the fund.

This performance dip results in a difference between the returns reported by the mutual funds and the returns earned by the funds' individual investors. Mutual fund returns for each period being measured are treated equally, "time-weighted," which means without regard to how much money was invested. The stellar returns reported before the monies flowed into a five-star rated fund are weighted the same as the returns after the mutual fund received the new money. Investor returns are calculated differently. Described as an internal rate of return or "dollar weighted," these calculations are based on the timing of these cash flows. Morningstar reports the relationship between the funds' returns and the investors' returns as a "success ratio."

Let me illustrate how this works.

Investor's Account					Return	
Beginning Value	Money In (out)	Return (Loss)	(Taxes)	Ending Value	Fund	Investor
	1,000	100	(10)	1,090	10.0%	9.0%
1,090	1,000	105	(11)	2,184	5.0%	4.5%
2,184	(1,000)	118	(12)	1,290	10.0%	9.0%
Dollar-weighted return - Earned by Investor						6.8%
Divided by						
Time-weighted return - Reported by Fund					8.3%	
Equals						
Success Ratio						82

(6.8% ÷ 8.3% = 82% or a success ratio of 82)

Illustration 4–9. The success ratio compares the returns reported by mutual funds with an estimate of the return investors earn after taxes and adjustments for when funds flowed into and out of the mutual funds.

Since 1994, *Dalbar*, a highly regarded financial industry rating service, has measured the effects of investor decisions to buy, sell, and switch into and out of mutual funds. "The results consistently show that the average investor earns less—in many cases, much less—than mutual fund performance reports would suggest."[25]

Further Confirmation of Poor(er) Results

In one study, John Bogle, founder and senior chairman of the Vanguard Group, reported that the return from the average equity mutual fund managed by professionals using Investing 1.0 was 83 percent of the market return.[26] In its "2016 Quantitative Analysis of Investor Behavior," Dalbar shows investors earning 58 percent of the S&P 500 from 2005 through 2015.

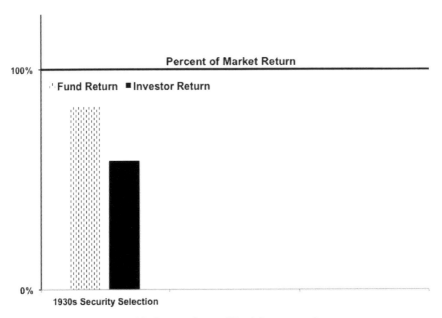

Illustration 4–10. Comparison of Bogle's report of average return of equity mutual fund using Investing 1.0 and Dalbar's Analysis of Investor Behavior showing average return of investors in those mutual funds, both as a percentage of market return. See Appendix A.

Recognizing the challenges faced by most investors, Nobel laureate Merton Miller said, "Most people might just as well buy a share of the whole market, which pools all the information, than delude themselves into thinking they know something the market doesn't."[27]

As noted previously, most of this book and the studies cited involve mutual funds and professional money managers because mutual funds publish data that enable studies of their investment performance. Individuals who invest in individual securities do not publish their investment performance and are not subject to the same regulatory controls.

That said, based on my experience reviewing investment portfolios constructed by individual investors, I have come to believe that most do worse than mutual funds managed by professionals using Investing 1.0—but they are not aware of their poor results. Why do they fare so poorly? First, they are ineffectively diversified. An example comes from a portfolio I reviewed that held shares in an S&P 500 index fund and also owned shares of a mutual fund that "*short*ed" the S&P 500. This short fund would gain value when the S&P 500 dropped in value. Because the returns from these two investments offset each other, after paying the mutual fund expenses and brokerage commissions, this investor always lost money by holding these offsetting positions. Others have invested too much in companies they were familiar with or worked for and too little in unfamiliar securities traded on foreign markets. Some contained too many stocks to consistently track and effectively manage. Also, many investors select mutual funds using methods that don't work very well, such as impressive, yet meaningless, sounding names or past performance. Too often these funds own many of the same stocks, what is known as overlap.

I have yet to find one of these investors employing a systematic method for selecting securities to buy and sell. Nor have I found one using a trading strategy that provides a competitive advantage over the professional traders. These shortcomings are not limited to investments in stocks. The fixed income securities in most of these portfolios fall short of the goals of maximum return for a given level of risk. By this I mean, some investors take on riskier fixed income investments because they expect to earn more, even though they could get a higher total portfolio return by buying more equity securities and balancing them with less risky bonds.

Lessons Learned

Those using Investing 1.0 fail to beat the market fundamentally because achieving all four conditions of superior performance is too difficult. Compounding this difficulty are natural instincts that frequently lead to a chain of mental errors that hamper our investing decisions. So what is an investor to do? Fortunately, as you'll read in the following chapters, others have already asked this question and found newer approaches that help to solve these problems.

CHAPTER 5

MODERN INVESTING

Before the less-than-stellar performance revealed the need for a more effective approach, Harry Markowitz, in 1952, challenged the common wisdom of the prior two decades that competent investors could pick three or four securities and beat the market by more than "a few small percentage points." He realized that picking a small number of securities did not account for the impact of risk. Asking a very unpopular question—"what if you're wrong?"—Markowitz developed a model that showed the risk of concentrating on only a few securities and the benefit of diversification.

Others followed Markowitz, adding criteria for guiding diversification and trading strategies that avoided paying too much when buying or getting too little when selling.

Markowitz Portfolio Selection (aka Modern Portfolio Theory)

What Markowitz proposed revolutionized the investment industry.[28] Diversification, the broader the better, could provide a "free lunch" by reducing risk without lowering expected returns. The best that an investor could do—that is, the highest expected return with the lowest standard deviation, which is the statistician's measure of risk—is bounded by a curve, as shown in Illustration 5–1. This curve is known as the "efficient frontier."

The use of the term "efficient" in "efficient market", "efficient market theory," and "efficient frontier" may confuse some readers. "Efficient market" and "efficient market theory" refer to how quickly new information is reflected in security prices and "efficient frontier" refers to the theoretical boundary of combinations of securities that give the best combination of risk and reward – highest return for a given level of risk or the lowest risk for a given level of expected return.

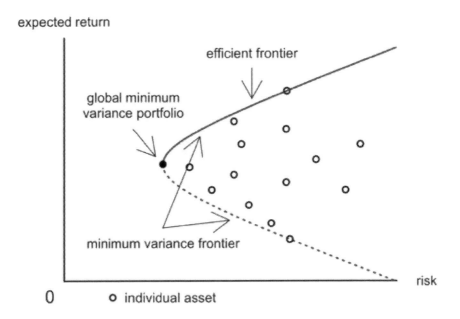

Illustration 5–1. Efficient frontier of risk and return.
(Source: Wikimedia Commons Minimum variance frontier of MPT)

One of the major insights of the Markowitz model is that it is a security's expected return, coupled with how its price changes relative to (co-varies with) other securities, that determines how to add it to a portfolio. The result of this insight is that investors can tailor a portfolio to their specific needs based on the securities they select and how those securities behave relative to the other securities in the portfolio. An investor who can live with more risk might choose a portfolio with a higher risk and expected return while a more risk-averse investor would be more likely to choose one with lower risk and expected return.

Capital Asset Pricing Model

Markowitz's theory sounded easy, but in order to use his portfolio selection process, investors needed a way to evaluate a security's price. Jack Treynor (1961), William F. Sharpe (1964), and John Lintner (1965) independently published such an evaluation method, known as the Capital Asset Pricing Model (CAPM).[29] CAPM focused on one thing: how closely the changes in the value of a security followed the changes in the value of the entire stock market. This pricing model made managing risk through diversification the key consideration when selecting securities.

Efficient Market

Despite Markowitz's portfolio theory and Sharpe's pricing model, the search continued for a more effective approach to find a systematic way to identify how to select securities. Those searching for the solution allayed their fear about being at a disadvantage to those who carefully studied individual securities when they found that new information was being so quickly incorporated into market prices that specialists in individual security selection no longer had a competitive advantage. This finding, the "efficient market theory," was identified by Gene Fama beginning with his PhD thesis in 1965.

Here's a basic definition of the efficient market: when many investors voluntarily agree to buy and sell securities, their trading reflects a vast amount of dispersed information. This trading drives prices. While new information may change the daily price, the efficient market theory accepts the stock price as an accurate estimate of current value, reflecting all known information about a company, including investor sentiment about it. Because they are not at risk to others trading with more current information, investors can profit from the efficiency, i.e. lower cost, of a systematic approach to security selection. Illustration 5–2 illustrates this funnel effect.

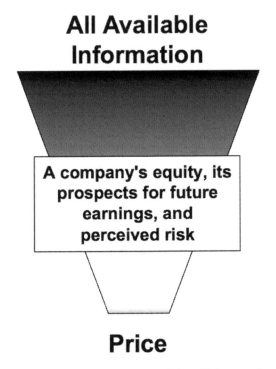

All Available Information

A company's equity, its prospects for future earnings, and perceived risk

Price

Illustration 5–2. An illustration of the efficient market.

Market efficiency discovered by Fama in 1965 is more powerful today than ever. Building on increasingly powerful computerized analysis and with the arrival of the Internet, we are now able to share new information quickly and cheaply, and prices adjust swiftly when unexpected events alter the market's view of the future.

Beyond Investing 1.0

Despite the theories developed by Markowitz, Sharpe and Fama, many investors continued to use Investing 1.0 as they "tried harder and hoped for the best." Investors' preference for this approach did not begin to change until the early 1970s, when low-cost index funds were introduced. I refer to the use of index funds as Investing 2.0.

The First Index Fund

The story behind the development of the first index fund starts with the president of Wells Fargo Bank in San Francisco, who was seeking to evaluate the investment performance for the bank's trust department's customers.[30] Ransom Cook and his successor, Richard Cooley, employed John "Mac" McQuown to use statistical analytics, similar to the methods Japanese automakers had used to improve their production process, to evaluate the bank's investment management.

Illustration 5–3. 1971 Datsun 280z. (Source: Wikimedia Commons. Datsun 280ZX Turbo in blue and silver, https://upload.wikimedia.org/wikipedia/commons/4/48/Datsun_280ZX_Turbo _in_blue_and_silver.jpg)

This 1971 Datsun 280z is an example of the Japanese application of statistical analytics to automobile production. By carefully reviewing the effectiveness of each step of the manufacturing process, Japanese manufacturers were able to produce cars with fewer defects at a lower cost.

After a great deal of research, development, and testing, McQuown and his team of finance scholars from MIT and the University of Chicago found that the returns generated by using Investing 1.0, both by the bank's trust department and from mutual funds, were not as good as the returns of the S&P 500. "Everybody thought it was easy to beat the S&P 500. It turns out, nobody was, or hardly anybody was, and certainly not consistently."[31]

This revelation led McQuown's team to an idea that would change the investment world: assume that all securities are fairly priced based upon their risk and relative to one another.[32] This enabled them to employ the concepts described in Markowitz' "Modern Portfolio Theory" and the single-factor CAPM to select investments. Assuming that stock and bond prices were fair, the McQuown team developed a systematic approach to building portfolios that would replace the method of one-by-one selection of individual securities. The story of how this came about is quite interesting.

In the late '60s, Keith Shwayder, whose family owned the Samsonite luggage company, worked at the University of Chicago as an assistant professor of accounting. When Shwayder discovered that the company pension fund was invested in mutual funds using Investing 1.0, he asked if anyone was managing money in the "theoretically proper" manner and was directed to the team at Wells Fargo. In 1971, Keith convinced his father to invest $6 million of the company pension fund into a fund created and managed at Wells Fargo. As a result, the first index fund—the Samsonite Luggage Fund—was born – and so was Investing 2.0.

The Samsonite Luggage Fund was based on an equal-weighted index of New York Stock Exchange equities. The fund worked, although there were heavy transaction costs and daily management was difficult (remember, this is the early days of computer applications to stock trading). In 1976, this strategy was replaced with a market-weighted strategy using the Standard & Poor's 500 Composite Stock Price Index.[33] This new strategy was first implemented in accounts run by Wells Fargo for its own pension fund and for Illinois Bell. Members of this team later influenced the creation of the first index fund available to the public, Vanguard's S&P 500 Index Fund.[34]

Today's index funds and **ETFs** like their forebear, the Samsonite Luggage Fund, allow a commercial index, such as the S&P 500, to determine which securities the fund will hold and when to trade them. Index funds prioritize tracking the index performance and avoid strategies that might perform differently from the index, even if the strategy could theoretically yield higher returns.

The success of index funds and ETFs can be attributed to their simplicity and low cost, as displayed in Illustration 5–4.

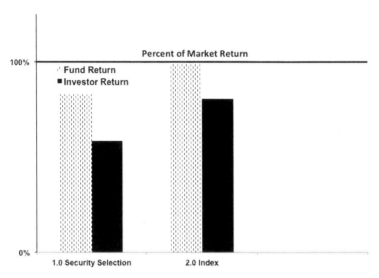

Illustration 5–4. Shows the comparison of returns from Investing 1.0 – individual security selection for a fund and returns from Investing 2.0 – indexing. See Appendix A.

We see this positive outcome in the investment performance of index funds and of their investors. Combining the analysis of Vanguard's John Bogle with information reported in Morningstar's Indexes Yearbook, we can see the advantage investors have gained from index funds and ETFs. Surpassing the average fund using Investing 1.0, the average index fund captured 99 percent of the market return.[35] More importantly, the *investors* in index funds did better than those investing in mutual funds that continue to employ Investing 1.0!

Using these two reports, we can piece together the picture that investors in mutual funds using Investing 1.0 captured 65 percent of the market return,[36] while investors in index funds captured 82 percent of the market return.[37] Quite a difference!

Looking behind these numbers, we find that index funds are generally more tax-efficient than mutual funds that use Investing 1.0. Plus, index fund investors are less likely to chase returns or to move in and out of index funds when compared to investors in individual stocks or funds using Investing 1.0.

A word of caution. More narrowly defined indexes, such as those targeting specific countries or sectors, such as health care, are a step backward toward Investing 1.0. They are based on forecast-based ideas of market-beating performance. Unfortunately, similar to Investing 1.0, they involve avoidable risks and too often miss the benefits of broad diversification. This, in turn, leads investors to chase returns by moving in and out of these very specialized index funds and ETFs.

While improvements in performance and returns have been good news for investors, the developers of the first index fund did not stop searching for better investment performance and looking even deeper into the forces that drive investment markets.

Lessons Learned

Index funds have consistently delivered superior performance when compared to the majority of mutual funds that select individual stocks for their portfolios, i.e., Investing 1.0. By harnessing advances in investment theory and employing computers to systematically evaluate investment performance, McQuown's team and the scholars from the University of Chicago and MIT found a practical application of the investment theories developed over the previous twenty years.

Because indexing replaces individual security selection with a systematic pricing model and introduces the trade-offs of risk and reward in portfolio design, it is two-dimensional, worthy of the label associated with a major software upgrade. Let's call it Investing 2.0.

CHAPTER 6

Beyond Market Indexes

As you saw, indexes provide a simple overview of investment markets, and index funds have proven to be a straightforward way for investors to capture market gains while avoiding the stress and risks associated with individual stock selection. But the researchers were not satisfied. They wanted to know how to earn more. Their study of historical market performance, enabled by the development of new forms of statistical analysis to study the inner workings of the markets, is referred to as quantitative research.

It has been evolving since 1900 when Louis Bachelier used advanced mathematics in his PhD thesis, *The Theory of Speculation*. Edgar Smith's 1924 analysis of historical performance of stocks and bonds, *Common Stocks as Long Term Investments*, you will recall from chapter 1, is another example of quantitative research. Despite its contribution to the 1929 Wall Street Crash, quantitative research continued.

After the Crash, in 1932 Alfred Cowles founded the Cowles Commission for Research in Economics. Its main contributions to economics include its creation and consolidation of two important fields that support statistical study of investment market behavior: general equilibrium theory and econometrics.

Research Using Computers

Beginning in 1960, researchers at the University of Chicago began building the Center for Research in Security Prices (CRSP) database. Using the CRSP database, researchers could perform statistical analysis on a sufficiently large data set to draw meaningful conclusions about investments and investment performance.

These scholars imposed scientific criteria on securities research. Similar to the standards set in other scientific fields, the findings must be documented, supported by evidence in markets around the world and across different time periods, and subject to peer review. To protect against the phenomenon known as data mining, the connection between cause and effect must make sense.

Initially, CRSP researchers measured historical performance of different types of investments. As shown in Illustration 6–1, the before-tax returns of T-bills have barely covered inflation, while longer-term bonds provided higher returns. Long-term returns of U.S. stocks have far exceeded inflation and significantly outperformed bonds. It is important to note, these performance metrics did not exist when Gerald Loeb proposed his ideas for beating the market or even during the early stages of professional money management in the 1940s and '50s. So these initial findings led to changes in our understanding of investing.

As these studies progressed, researchers moved beyond single-factor indexes to identify additional characteristics, resulting in systematic ways to identify stocks that provide higher than market average returns. For example, consider the performance of small cap stocks—which are the smallest market value companies whose stock is publicly traded on U.S. stock exchanges—versus *large cap stocks*—the largest publicly traded companies. From 1926 through 2016, the cumulative return from U.S. small cap stocks was more than *three times greater* than the return from U.S. large cap stocks.

Growth of a Dollar, 1926 – 2016
(Compounded monthly)

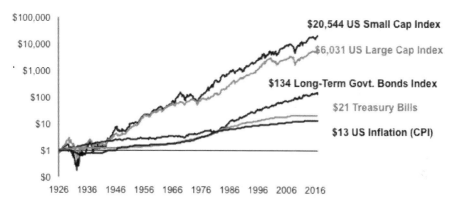

Illustration 6–1. Graph shows the growth of various investment vehicles from 1926–2016. (Source: Dimensional Fund Advisors, Master Slide Library Published March 25, 2017, PowerPoint Slide Number 4)

Again, many of these metrics were unknown in the first half of the 20th Century. When looking behind the numbers shown in Illustration 6–1, we see that higher returns come from investments that carry greater risk and uncertainty. *Treasury bills*, which are less risky than bonds or stocks, return less. Although this chart shows the higher long-term returns, concern about risk and uncertainty is often focused on short-term time horizons. As shown in Chapter 4, during shorter periods of time, there is no obvious pattern in returns that can be exploited for higher profits. Thus, short-term risk is often cited when making the case for broad diversification across many different types of investments, or *asset classes*.

All of these illustrations highlight the primary insights gained from the quantitative research: investment markets are constantly pricing securities to reflect a positive expected return going forward, and returns often vary from what is expected.

Research Beyond Indexing

Another example of the progress that has been made is the series of advances since the Capital Asset Pricing Model (CAPM) was published in the 1960's. At that time, there was little data available and computers had relatively little power for analyzing more complex elements involved in investment behavior. Since then, as computer-processing power has increased and more comprehensive data has become available, the researchers have tested the limits of the CAPM.

While some of the research validated Sharpe's pricing model, other studies developed a more complete understanding of how investment markets work and how investors get rewarded for taking risks. Some of the most widely cited studies found that smaller company stocks have larger returns than large company stocks,[38] stocks with higher ratios of book value to market value have larger returns than stocks with lower ratios,[39] and profitable firms generate higher returns than unprofitable ones.[40] Because these researchers reasoned that the first two factors of higher returns are compensation for higher risks, they refer to the differences as "risk factors" or "factors" for short. Importantly, these factors provide a more precise method for guiding an investment portfolio's asset allocation.

I prefer this research to what is promoted by Wall Street analysts and financial pundits because these studies were published by, and have withstood peer review by, prominent economists including some who have been recognized with the Nobel Prize in economics.

How Much Higher?

Risk Factors	Increase in Annual Return
	1928 - 2016
Market Stocks vs bonds	8.10%
Company Size Small vs large companies	3.91%
Relative Price Value vs growth companies	4.65%
	1964 - 2016
Profitability High vs low profitability companies	3.76%

Illustration 6–2. Risk factors help determine an investment portfolio's asset allocation.

Fixed Income Investments

Although most of this book is focused on investing in stocks—also called equity securities—the trade-off between risk and reward also affects bonds, which are fixed income securities. The primary factors that drive differences in expected returns for fixed income securities are the term—the time until you get your money back—and credit worthiness—the risk that you won't get paid back on time or at all[41].

The mechanics of calculating expected return of fixed income securities involve only two elements: current return (*coupon rate* divided by current price) and change in price. Because many fixed income securities differ only by term, the market tells us how much to expect the price to change. This is known as the *yield curve*. While many pundits forecast changes in interest rates and security prices, extensive research has found that investors are better off simply relying on the current yield curve to make their decisions.

Lessons Learned

Investing 2.0, indexing, is based on the Capital Asset Pricing Model's single-factor view of portfolio construction that relies on how closely the changes in the value of individual securities follow the changes in the value of the entire stock market. To many, this seemed overly simplistic. Subsequent research, which systematically identified stocks expected to generate higher returns, confirmed that the single factor view was, in fact, too simplistic.

CHAPTER 7

THE SECRET SAUCE

T aking the advances incorporated in index funds several steps forward requires other breakthroughs. As described in Chapter 6,
one step replaces index fund reliance solely on indexes to guide
in security selection with newly identified pricing factors. These pricing
factors highlight the relationship between higher than average expected
returns and riskier investments. Other steps include integrating trading
strategies with portfolio design and constantly monitoring to incorporate the latest evidence-based research.

Illustration 7–1. Tesla Model X. (Source: Wikimedia Commons)

These new advances in investing can be compared to the 2016 Tesla Model X—an example of state-of-the-art integration of technology and automotive design that is revolutionary to the auto industry. These vehicles continue to evolve even after they leave the factory because Tesla incorporates the latest design features through remotely distributed software modifications.

Because new advances in investing replace the single-factor pricing model used by index funds with a multi-factor pricing model, integrate trading strategies with portfolio design, and are constantly updating to incorporate the latest evidence-based research, this approach represents the third generation of investing. It is multi-dimensional, worthy of a label associated with a major software upgrade: "Investing 3.0."

Portfolio Construction 3.0

Significant investment research has centered on the process for selecting investments, deciding which ones to buy or sell and how much of each one to own. Investors who employ the latest research underlying Investing 3.0 start with the universe of all publicly traded securities and use filters to exclude those that do not fit the desired risk / reward profile. For example, utility stocks are excluded from value stock strategies because they behave differently from those in other types of companies classified as "value stocks," and their returns have been historically lower.

This research has stretched out over several decades, and each finding adds to the body of knowledge while building on what came before.

As we saw in Chapter 5, the Capital Asset Pricing Model (CAPM), a single factor model, was developed in the 1960s.

Single-Factor Model
(1963)

Market

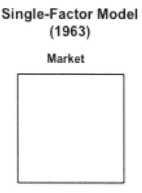

**Illustration 7–2. Capital Asset Pricing Model
(CAPM) view of investment markets**

Subsequent tests found that higher returns of stock of smaller companies could not be explained by CAPM. Small cap stocks provide a dimension that should be considered during portfolio construction.

Size Effect
(1981)

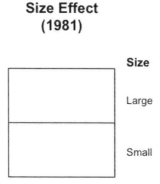

Illustration 7–3. View of investment markets showing Size Effect.

Additional research found that value stocks, defined by the ratio of a company's net book value to its market value, behaved differently and, similar to small cap stocks, should be considered during portfolio construction.

Value Effect
(1991)

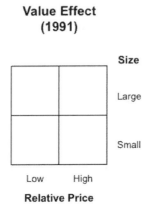

Illustration 7–4. In research published in 1993, Fama and French expanded the number of dimensions, described as risk factors, that capture long-term market premiums.

Most recently, research has identified a company's profitability, before special accounting adjustments, as another factor to be considered during portfolio construction.

Profitability
(2012)

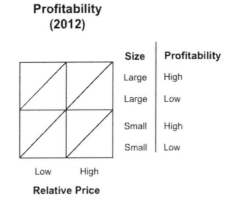

Illustration 7-5. View of investment markets showing integration of Size, Value, and Profitability premiums.

Researchers found that each factor is affected by other factors. A higher expected return, referred to as a "premium," might appear large when studied in isolation, but it often has a smaller impact when combined with others. For example, you cannot simply add size and relative price premiums together to find the premium on a small-value portfolio.

Avoid Style Drift

Having spent time and effort constructing a portfolio that effectively captures expected market premiums while limiting exposure to risks, investors then need to maintain the balance between risk and reward. One problem investors face occurs when the market value of a company changes, which is referred to as "size", or when securities change in relative price or some other characteristic of risk and reward. Professional investors refer to this as "style drift," which can cause problems for managers if they do not monitor the changes and make necessary adjustments or if they chase opportunities in other types of securities, such as a stock manager buying bonds.

Institutional investors, such as large corporate pension plans or major charitable foundations, are more forgiving of managers whose returns are less than expected than they are of managers who allow style drift. Why? Institutional investors hire many managers, each with a specific expertise and don't want one manager duplicating the efforts of another or failing to provide the desired allocation. When I was the CFO at RREEF, we were hired to invest in real estate, only real estate.

Style drift is a problem for Investing 2.0 index funds because the indexes infrequently change the securities included or the size of their holdings, even when the securities change in size or relative price. Whatever its causes, style drift introduces inconsistent exposure to investment risk and expected performance.

In contrast, those who have moved beyond Investing 2.0 index funds to Investing 3.0 use asset allocation as a way to enforce style discipline, that is, to ensure that they have consistent exposure to the key risk / reward factors, to guide their trading strategies.

Trading Strategies

Portfolio construction methods influence trading costs, and trading costs influence the returns that portfolios are able to deliver. For example, it would not make sense to pursue an expected higher return of 4 percent if it costs 4.5 percent to capture. Premiums that require a portfolio to be turned over several times per year can be difficult to capture on an after-cost basis.

Historically, higher returning securities were the most costly to trade. Before the introduction of Investing 3.0, high trading costs discouraged investors from developing strategies that captured market premiums.

The developers of index funds understood this and concentrated on securities with the lowest trading costs.

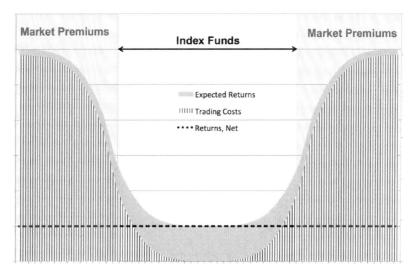

Illustration 7–6. Similar to investors and mutual fund managers who build portfolios one security at a time, index funds use trading strategies that emphasize immediacy over price. Demanding immediacy "costs" more when transacting in smaller-cap securities or more volatile value stocks. The increase in the vertically lined area depicts the higher trading costs these investors face. Higher trading costs offset the return premiums investors expect from these securities. Because index funds gain little from pursuing market premiums, index funds limit the securities they track to those that can be traded at low cost.

The team involved in developing the Investing 3.0 approach understood that effective trading strategies were required to deliver these market premiums to investors. By incorporating cost effective trading strategies, they were able to expand the reach of their mutual funds and capture the market premiums that elude index funds.

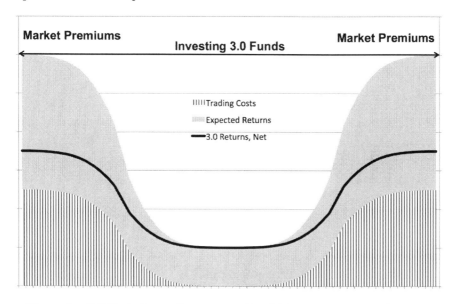

Illustration 7–7. Reducing trading costs enables 3.0 investors to expand into areas where they can capture the expected premiums of small and value stocks.

Exploit Trading Advantages

When the scholars moved beyond Investing 2.0 to Investing 3.0, they turned tart lemons into sweet lemonade by emphasizing strategies that minimized trading costs. Their breakthrough came from adopting flexible trading strategies that turned the cost of demanding liquidity into a benefit—by providing liquidity.

Let's go back and remember what drives the demand for liquidity. Index fund reconstitution is similar to investment portfolio trades that are driven by Investing 1.0's focus on individual securities. Both require traders to execute buy and sell instructions of specific securities. Most often these are time-sensitive trades that require immediate action, and the traders have limited flexibility to lessen the transaction costs.

In contrast to the urgency and inflexibility of the trading strategies employed by traders using Investing 1.0 and by Investing 2.0 index funds, patience and flexibility are incorporated into Investing 3.0. Traders using Investing 3.0 strategies improve liquidity because they are flexible in what they buy and when. Because their systematic approach is based on key financial data, traders of securities in flexible portfolios substitute difficult-to-trade securities with similar ones available on more attractive terms. Without the "need to get done" constraints imposed by indexed or traditional portfolios, these fund traders can enhance portfolio returns by taking advantage of traders who have more limited flexibility, such as those with index funds that must reconstitute. They can then couple this flexibility with the willingness to break trades into smaller pieces that stretch over longer time periods, reducing trading costs of each trade.

To execute these strategies, investors need traders who are dedicated to getting the best execution for the investment client and avoiding conflicts of interest with in-house accounts. The traders need to trade in markets selected for lowest costs, including taxes, and have simultaneous access to multiple markets. Needless to say, this capability is expensive and generally unavailable to individual investors.

Improving on Trading Strategies Used by Investing 2.0 Index Funds

Index funds' strict adherence to tracking indexes comes at a cost in the form of reduced discretion around trading. Most indexes revise their list of securities annually or quarterly, and securities may be added or deleted from the index at that time. This process is referred to as index reconstitution.

For example, when the annual reconstitution of the widely tracked Russell indexes occurred on June 24, 2016, funds tracking the Russell indexes needed to buy stocks that were added to the index and sell stocks that were deleted from the indexes they tracked in order to minimize fund tracking error relative to the index. Any deviation of the fund from the index, over days or even hours, could result in different returns from the index, which is referred to as *tracking error*. Because the mission of index funds is to track the performance of an index, tracking error is considered undesirable.

As you might imagine, other investors try to profit from knowing what trades the index funds will make. They drive up the prices of securities that the index funds will buy and drive down the prices of securities the index funds will sell. Because of high liquidity demands around index reconstitution dates, index funds may incur high trading costs that do not appear in expense ratios but do affect their net returns. In other words, the funds' goal of minimizing tracking error may come at the expense of returns.

Minimize Trading Activity

The more complexity an investor uses to construct an investment portfolio, the more expensive it becomes in terms of turnover and other transaction costs. Recognizing this, Investing 3.0's strategy weighs those costs against the benefits of maintaining a well-diversified portfolio and the desired exposure to the risk / reward factors.

Impact on Individual Investors

While these descriptions of alternate strategies may sound interesting, what really matters is how investors fare when they go beyond Investing 2.0 indexing and use Investing 3.0.

The first benefit to using Investing 3.0 is the ability to customize the balance between risk and reward. Because these refinements bring risk into the conversation about portfolio design, Investing 3.0 helps investors more precisely select the combinations of risk and reward that they feel most comfortable with.

Recent Results

Investing 3.0 has sufficient history for investors to review results. The table in Illustration 7–8 shows a series of mutual funds that employ Investing 3.0. Most beat their corresponding benchmarks. This table shows ten years, from April 1, 2007, thru March 31, 2017. If you stretch the period out further, to include the entire life of each of these funds, the picture looks even better. These positive results don't happen with 1970s style index funds, which are designed to return their benchmarks less operating expenses. And, as we saw with Investing 1.0, no one, including Bernie Madoff, can reliably forecast the market's direction or predict which stock, fund, or investment manager will outperform.

Fund	Benchmark Index	Value at March 31, 2016 of $1,000 Invested April 1, 2007		
		Fund	Index	%
Emerging Markets Core Equity	MSCI Emerging Mkts (net div.)	1,470	1,310	112%
International Core Equity	MSCI World ex USA (net div.)	1,210	1,120	108%
International Small Cap Value	MSCI World ex USA Small Cap (net div.)	1,390	1,310	106%
International Value	MSCI World ex USA (net div.)	1,040	1,120	93%
US Core Equity 1	Russell 3000	2,090	2,070	101%
US Core Equity 2	Russell 3000	2,010	2,070	97%
US Large Cap Value	Russell 1000 Value	1,910	1,780	107%
US Micro Cap	Russell 2000	2,040	1,990	103%
US Small Cap Value	Russell 2000 Value	1,850	1,810	102%
AVERAGE				103%

Illustration 7–8. Although the returns from mutual funds employing Investing 3.0 are often better than mutual funds using Investing 1.0 and 2.0, there are times when market conditions work against them and they do not outperform corresponding benchmarks as you can see for the International Value fund and the US core Equity 2 fund. Source: Dimensional Fund Advisors Returns Web, May 8, 2017.

Updated Pricing Model

Investing 3.0 incorporates the additional pricing factors and employs the advanced, less costly trading strategies. Mutual funds using Investing 3.0 have delivered higher returns than their Investing 2.0 index fund counterparts, which, in turn, have delivered higher returns than funds managed by professionals focused on Investing 1.0 individual security selection.

While this analysis provides a compelling picture of better investment performance, it doesn't show the full benefit investors enjoy after they move beyond Investing 2.0 indexing to Investing 3.0. The expanded pricing model facilitates an understanding of asset allocation and how to look at market volatility. Those who embrace it behave as contrarians by moving into types of investments whose values have dropped and out of others after the values have risen. In 2005 Morningstar reported the success ratio for the investors in these funds at 109 percent of the funds' returns.

Illustration 7–9 shows in simple terms that newer knowledge about how the markets work has led to strategies for investing that are paying off.

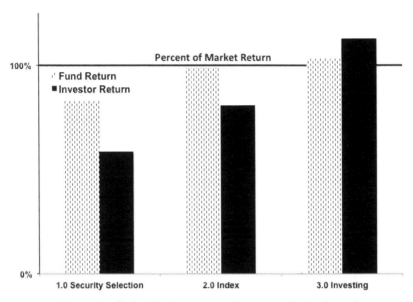

Illustration 7–9. This chart shows the returns for the investing approaches discussed in this book. See Appendix A.

Lessons Learned

Investing 3.0 integrates advanced concepts of portfolio construction with strategies that minimize trading costs, which enables investors to capture higher returns than those using Investing 2.0 index funds or Investing 1.0 strategies.

Although you may feel encouraged to learn how markets have evolved and to know that you can profit from investment scholars' deeper under-standing of investment markets, you likely are reading this book because you want to learn how to make more money from investing. To learn how you can profit from using Investing 3.0, let's move to the next chapter.

CHAPTER 8

How You Can Profit

As you have learned in this book, steady advances in our understanding of investing have provided new ways to harness the power of modern investment markets. In this chapter, you learn how to create and maintain an investment plan that allows you to profit from the most recent advances.

Create an Investment Plan

Before the introduction of Investing 2.0 index funds, portfolios were built one security at a time. Assuming the investor had an advisor or broker, the investor assumed that the advisor had special expertise and knew best. Due to limited information, an investor could do little to "instruct" the investment advisor. While chief financial officer of RREEF, I saw how institutional investors selected their professional investment advisors; this framework was a long way from "expecting them to pick stocks." This chapter presents a simplified version of the communication that I observed.

Start with a written investment plan, which serves as a reference for everyone involved in your investments. If you use a professional advisor, the investment plan, sometimes referred to as an investment policy statement (IPS), serves as an instruction manual. Once established, it is then the investment advisor's role to follow your policy. Maintaining the IPS is the responsibility of both parties.

The IPS should describe your investment goals, such as how much money you will need and when you will need it, what kinds of risks you will tolerate and which ones you want to avoid, and the returns you expect. While many investors may say the sky's the limit, you shouldn't. A discussion about risks is an important step in developing your investment plan.

I generally recommend that clients avoid the following risks:

- Insufficient diversification that occurs if you invest in a limited number of securities or over concentrate in selected markets, such as U.S. only, or a limited number of asset classes.
- Strategies that involve the risks associated with Investing 1. 0, including economic forecasting, market timing, or proprietary "research".
- Proprietary investment strategies that lack transparency or a review by independent professionals.
- Private investment programs with limited secondary markets that lack transparency and provide few investor protections.
- Derivatives or other financial instruments that are speculative in nature, lack transparency, and are not based on broad economic factors.
- Short selling: selling securities you don't own and must buy some time in the future.
- Using borrowed funds, known as margin.

The most important part of the nuts and bolts section of your plan deals with how much you want to invest in different types of investments, i.e., asset allocation. When you're looking to invest in real estate, you will often hear that the most important considerations are "*location, location, location.*" When you're creating your investment plan, the most important consideration is asset allocation.

Once you have established your IPS, don't change it until there is a material change in your financial circumstances or another type of significant event that would prompt you to revise it. Don't alter it in response to articles you read, "experts" you hear, or changing market conditions. The plan should be long-term to prevent arbitrary or impulsive revisions. I can't emphasize this enough: *maintaining discipline and dedica-tion to your long-term investment strategies are critical to your investment success.*

Maintain Your Investment Plan

Creating an investment plan takes you part way toward your invest-ment goals. To complete the journey, you need to maintain your plan. Just like exercise is the key to getting in shape or a diet is necessary to weight loss, your plan is the key to keeping you on the path to your investment goals.

Rebalancing

If your plan is based on a pricing model that balances risk and reward, maintaining your asset allocation maintains your plan's balance. Start with the preferred allocation identified in your plan and consider how far you will allow, say, each asset class to drift, which is known as a toler-ance band. The asset allocation needs to be monitored at least monthly and when an asset class percentage exceeds the maximum or drops be-low the minimum tolerance band, you should buy and sell to align the asset classes with the preferred allocation. This process is known as re-balancing. Although some firms rebalance at specified times—such as each quarter or once a year—I have found that using tolerance bands is more effective and avoids unnecessary costs.

Taxes

Your investment plan should consider how to minimize your income taxes and capital gains taxes. The first step is to select mutual funds that minimize trading activity, which triggers capital gains that are passed on to their investors.

The next step is to choose which investments to place in your tax-de-ferred accounts, such as a 401(k), 403(b) or IRA, and which investments to place in taxable accounts. This is known as tax location. Investments such as interest-bearing, fixed-income securities and shares of real estate investment trusts (REITs) trigger a higher U.S. government tax rate and should be held in tax-deferred accounts. The investments you expect to have the highest long-term growth should be held in Roth IRAs.

The third step comes when you select shares of mutual funds to sell. You should keep track of how much you pay each time you buy shares. This is referred to as by "lot." When you sell shares held in taxable accounts, you should select them using the following criteria:

(1) Short-term losses: lots resulting in short-term losses are sold first, from largest short-term loss to smallest short-term loss

(2) Long-term losses: lots resulting in long-term losses are sold, from largest long-term loss to smallest long-term loss

(3) Short-term, no gains or losses: short-term lots reflecting no gain or loss

(4) Long-term, no gains or losses: long-term lots reflecting no gain or loss

(5) Long-term gains: lots resulting in long-term gains are sold from smallest long-term gain to largest long-term gain

(6) Short-term gains: lots resulting in short-term gains are sold from smallest short-term gain to largest short-term gain.

Selling shares to report short-term or long-term losses is referred to as "loss harvesting" when done separate from rebalancing.

Operating costs

You should avoid fees, transaction costs, and other expenses that are not justified by realistic objectives of your investment plan. Instead, seek out investment strategies that minimize portfolio turnover and the related trading, income taxes, and other operating costs. Whether you take command of your investments or hire a professional, you need to make sure this is a smooth ride, like one with an experienced ship captain navigating a winding river. You don't want someone acting like Walt Disney's Steamboat Willie, swinging the wheel wildly from one side to another to avoid running aground; you want someone who sets an effective course and makes only minor adjustments as the course requires.

Monitor Performance

To make sure your investments continue to be consistent with the invest-ment objectives, goals, and guidelines of your IPS, you must measure the performance of your portfolio, as well as asset class components, against commonly accepted performance benchmarks. Such bench-marks include:

- BofA Merrill Lynch 1-Year US Treasury Note Index
- Citi World Government Bond Index 1–2 Years (hedged to USD)
- Citi World Government Bond Index 1–5 Years (hedged to USD)
- CRSP US Mid Cap Index
- CRSP US Small Cap Growth Index
- CRSP US Small Cap Index
- CRSP US Small Cap Value Index
- CRSP US Total Market Index
- Dow Jones US Select REIT Index
- MSCI Emerging Markets Index (net div.)
- MSCI World ex USA Index (net div.)
- Russell 1000 Value Index
- Russell 2000 Value Index
- Russell 3000 Index
- Russell 3000 Value Index

Fama and others who have pioneered the investment theories behind investment performance recommend appropriate benchmarking as cru-cial to meaningful evaluation of investment performance.

Do It Yourself or Hire a Professional Advisor?

What is the best way for you to implement and maintain your investment plan? As you read in chapter 4, investors are often their own worst en-emies. I've heard some people question the value of a professional advi-sor by saying, "If no one can beat the market, I can just own index funds and avoid the cost of a professional advisor." They believe the role of an investment advisor is to select investment securities and buy or sell when the time is right. Because frequent buying and selling is costly and has been proven to be harmful to an investor's financial health, some believe they are better off following a strategy to buy and hold individual securities or an index fund that captures the average return of the total market.

Recognizing this, Vanguard has listed strategies that advisors employ to deliver as "Advisor Alpha."[42] Alpha is financial industry slang for returns above market returns and, consistent with the success ratio described in Illustration 7–5, Vanguard estimates that Advisor Alpha can exceed 3 percent per year. The ways advisors deliver alpha include:

- Suitable asset allocation using broadly diversified funds, ETFs
- Cost-effective implementation
- Rebalancing
- **Behavioral coaching**
- Asset location
- Withdrawal order
- Total return versus income investing

Although almost everyone is *capable* of taking the steps to effectively implement and maintain their own investment plan, from what I have seen, few *will* take those steps. In fact, most won't and should hire a professional advisor who will.

Furthermore, if you have read this far, it may be apparent to you by now that that many investors do not realize there are investing strategies that could be earning them the higher returns identified by world renown scholars. Out of either lack of knowledge of how the investment world has changed or fear of making a change they continue on, likely earning a respectable return but less than what is possible.

Behavioral Coaching

Among the strategies listed above, Vanguard highlights behavior coaching as having an impact that is significantly greater than any of the other strategies. Behavioral coaching provides something impossible for you to gain on your own: an independent perspective. Even when your investment strategy is in place, doubts and fears will inevitably arise. At this point, your advisor becomes your coach, reinforcing the principles behind your plan and keeping you on track.

Your advisor will listen to your fears, tease out the issues driving those feelings, and provide practical, long-term solutions. Your advisor will scan the horizon for issues that may affect you and keep you informed about potential problems or upcoming opportunities.

Time and Access

Two benefits not listed in Vanguard's description of Advisor Alpha are how professional advisors can save you time and can provide access to higher-performing institutional investment products that employ Investing 3.0 strategies.

Most of us have many demands on our time. If you prefer spending your time and attention on your job or your family or your hobbies, then you should consider hiring a professional advisor who will save you the time and effort required to manage your investments.

There is another important difference that an advisor can bring – access. While mutual funds with the lowest operating expenses often limit access through large minimum investments, the leading mutual fund manager using Investing 3.0 strategies limits access to its funds to institutional investors or investment advisors who have passed a rigorous screening process. They expect these professionals to behave in ways that will contribute to the success of their investment strategy as well as to their clients' success.

Selecting an Investment Advisor

If you decide to engage an investment advisor, establish criteria for selecting such a professional. First and foremost, consider how effectively the advisor will implement your policies, particularly those involving risks and allowable investments. The advisor should employ Investing 3.0: incorporate ongoing scientific research, build investment portfolios based on advanced research, and employ desired trading and rebalancing techniques as described in Vanguard's Advisor's Alpha. Anyone doing less should be avoided.

Require the advisor to be an independent registered investment advisor (RIA), to avoid conflicts of interest, and to commit in writing to put your interests first, which is known as serving as a *fiduciary*.

John Bowen, CEO of CEG Worldwide, an advisor to leading wealth managers, says you should look for an advisor with what he calls the six C's: character, chemistry, caring, competence, cost-effective, and consultative.[43] At first glance, each of these C's appears individually subjective, without a common distinction. However, there is a way to distinguish competence.

One measure of an advisor's competence is how often their recommendations perform as well as expected. Most advisors using Investing 1.0 employ a process for replacing underperforming mutual funds. Standard practice is to use a "watch list". Although a watch list is intended to convey diligence in monitoring investment performance, it doesn't. Having a watch list means that the advisor has recommended too many investments that have not performed as well as expected.

Why is this a problem? Beyond the obvious problem with disappointing investment performance, if too many of your advisor's recommendations underperform, you are less likely to follow his/her advice, particularly at times when you need it the most, such as the peaks and valleys in the emotional curve of investing (Illustration 4-8).

I have found the systematic approach of Investing 3.0 avoids the need for a watch list and reinforces my clients' confidence in my recommendations.

Evaluating Your Advisor

Similar to the steps you must take to maintain your investment plan, you also need to take steps to evaluate your advisor's performance. These evaluations should be done at least annually and can be measured by the following criteria:

1. Investment performance
2. Adherence to your investment plan, including investment selection and associated risks
3. Qualitative changes to the investment manager's organization

Lessons Learned

To get the most benefit from Investing 3.0, you need to employ discipline. Starting with creating an investment plan that describes your investment goals and the risks you will tolerate, you need to clearly document the characteristics of your investments and investment approach.

This discipline includes maintaining your investment portfolio by doing what Vanguard describes as "Advisor Alpha." Although most investors are capable of undertaking the efforts that, according to Vanguard's estimates, will increase returns by 3 percent per year, few do. Importantly, professional advisors offer critical benefits that individuals cannot realize on their own: saving time and providing an independent perspective.

CHAPTER 9

CONCLUSION

Over the past 100 years, modern investing has made enormous strides. Like a phoenix rising out of the ashes of the Wall Street Crash of 1929, investment markets became a place where each investor could earn his or her share of the market's returns. As the understanding of investing has progressed, so has investor success.

Starting in the 1930s with an approach based on individual security selection, modern investing has made significant progress. In the 1970s, index funds began using advances in computers and computerized databases to couple a systematic approach to security selection with portfolio design. Beginning in the 1980s and continuing through today, the developers of the first index funds have improved on their initial design, taking advantage of increasingly powerful computers and databases to add new research to their approach. They have expanded their pricing model for improved performance—emphasizing securities expected to deliver higher than market average returns and more effective balancing of risk and return. They have incorporated advanced trading strategies into portfolio construction and developed a process for adopting new findings that help deliver better performance. The performance of Investing 3.0 demonstrates that these advances are paying off with better results.

Financial advisors trained in Investing 3.0 are helping individuals benefit from these advances. Their guidance helps investors avoid costly purchases that fail to deliver market returns and can protect investors from themselves—steering them away from mistakes that occur when emotions are allowed to sabotage investment decisions.

These advances in trading strategies can help investors capture more of the potential the investment markets can deliver.

Just as scientific research has led to advances in medicine, financial market research has led to major advances in investing. Major advances that can help *you* become a more successful investor. You now know how Investing 3.0 takes advantage of the investment markets—rather than letting the investment markets take advantage of you.

If you're susceptible to those who would profit at your expense, find a qualified investment advisor who is expert in Investing 3.0 to help you create a plan and portfolio that will allow you to take full advantage going forward of what the markets have to offer!

APPENDIX A

COMPARISON OF INVESTMENT PERFORMANCE

The comparisons shown in Illustration 4-10, Illustration 5-4, and Illustration 7-7 highlight the benefits investors have gained from breakthroughs in our understanding of investments and investment markets. As you have read, investments and investment markets behave differently at different times. Because these benefits vary over time, these illustrations show the relative benefits of each investment approach and the relationship between investment returns reported by mutual funds and those earned by individual investors.

Despite a lack of precision, these differences are noteworthy. They meet the criteria for scientific research. They have been found in markets throughout the world and at many different times. Importantly, there are sensible reasons to believe investors should take them into account when selecting an investment approach.

For example, in 1999 John Bogle, founder of Vanguard Mutual Funds, reported that from 1984 through 1998 the average mutual fund using Investing 1.0 (1930s approach) to select securities reported a pre-tax return of 13.6 percent, versus the total stock market return of 16.4 percent or 83 percent of market. The after-tax return of the average equity mutual fund was 10.6 percent or 65 percent of market.[44]

Although there have been few studies similar to Bogle's, I have pieced together a picture of these relationships. Dalbar's Quantitative Analysis of Investor Behavior for the period ended December 31, 2015 reports that for the prior ten years, the average equity fund investor's return was 4.23 percent or 58 percent of the S&P 500 return of 7.31 percent.[45]

When looking at the returns for index funds, we start again with Bogle's 1999 report. He reported that an all U.S. market index fund returned 16.2 percent before tax and 15.2 percent after tax[46] or 99 percent and 93 percent, respectively, of the market return. Each is a significant improvement over mutual funds using Investing 1.0 securities selection.

Using the Morningstar Indexes Yearbook 2005, we see that the average annual return from 1996 through 2005 for all no-load index funds was 8.65 percent[47] or 94 percent of the US market return for that period. The Morningstar Indexes Yearbook 2005 reports the success ratio for 2.0 Index fund investors to be 82.[48] Although less than what Bogle had reported, these results are significantly better than the before tax returns of mutual funds using Investing 1.0 securities selection.

Continuing with the Morningstar Indexes Yearbook 2005, we learn that the average annual return for funds using Investing 3.0 was 9.9 percent or 108 percent of market. This above market return is similar to what I show in illustration 7-6. Remarkably, Morningstar goes on to report that investors in Investing 3.0 funds enjoyed a success ratio of 109[49], which was 53% better than 2.0 Index fund investors.

A word of caution. The Morningstar study occurred during a period when there was a high benefit to rebalancing and this success ratio is higher than you would expect during other times. Because the success ratio is applied to individual mutual funds only, it differs from what would be reported for a portfolio of mutual funds across different asset classes.

APPENDIX B

WHAT IT MEANS TO BE A PRUDENT INVESTOR

In my ongoing research into what makes a successful investor, I explored what others had learned and shared along the way. In addition to the history of quantitative research and why it matters, I explored how the legal profession has shaped investing. As you read in chapter 3, the laws enacted in response to the Wall Street Crash of 1929 provided the framework for today's financial industry.

Legal and Customary Standards
An extension of the framework established by the federal government after 1929 is a legal standard based on what really smart and experienced investors do with their own money. These often come from court cases, laws, or regulations.

Prudent Man Rule
The "Prudent Man Rule" was established in 1830 by the Massachusetts Supreme Court in the case of *Harvard College v. Amory*. The key phrase:

> observe how men of prudence, discretion and intelligence manage their own affairs, not in regard to speculation, but in regard to the permanent disposition of their funds, considering the

probable income, as well as the probable safety of the capital to be invested.

Legal List Rule

Over the years, various court decisions took the broad Prudent Man Rule and converted it into narrow rules that classified investments on a stand-alone basis. In 1869, the New York Court of Appeals in *King v. Talbot* interpreted this standard to mean that only government bonds and mortgage-backed corporate debt were "prudent." This approach is known as the "Legal List Rule," and variations of this list were adopted by a majority of the states.

Prudent Man Rule II

However, changing business and economic conditions in the U.S. led eventually to the decline of the Legal List Rule. In 1942, the Prudent Man Rule statute was drafted by the National Conference of Commissioners on Uniform State Laws (NCCUSL) to overcome the unintended consequences of the Legal List Rule. Known as "Prudent Man Rule II," it adopted some language of the original:

> a fiduciary shall exercise the judgment and care, under the circumstances then prevailing, which men of prudence, discretion and intelligence exercise in the management of their own affairs, not in regard to speculation but in regard to the permanent disposition of their funds, considering the probable income as well as the probable safety of their capital.

The Prudent Man Rule II gained judicial and legislative popularity across the U.S. and came to dominate American trust law.

Second Restatement

In 1959, the NCCUSL restated the rule [Section 227 of the Restatement (Second) of Trusts] to make trust assets productive by seeking the highest possible income while preserving the nominal value of the principal. This came to be known as the "Second Restatement."

Subsequent to the publication of the Second Restatement in 1959, legal experts came to recognize that inflation threatened the purchasing power of a portfolio's principal. The preference for current income over appreciation in value caused many to view the Prudent Man Rule as an overly conservative method to protect trust administrators at the expense of trust beneficiaries.

Additionally, the growing body of theoretical and empirical research by financial economists, known as Modern Portfolio Theory, was becoming more widely accepted as an investment management technique by professional money managers. These findings exposed concepts restricting trust assets to certain investments as inadequate and even harmful to the interests they were designed to protect.

ERISA

In 1974, Congress enacted the Employee Retirement Income Security Act (ERISA) to protect the retirement plans of *private sector* employees. ERISA moved beyond the Second Restatement, as it codified language similar to Prudent Man Rule II that a fiduciary shall discharge its duties "with the care, skill, prudence, and diligence under the circumstances then prevailing that a prudent man acting in a like capacity and familiar with such matters would use in the conduct of an enterprise of like character and like aims."

Additionally, it took into account Modern Portfolio Theory in directing fiduciaries to discharge their duties "by diversifying the investments of the plan so as to minimize the risk of large losses, unless under the circumstances it is clearly prudent not to do so."

Restatement Third: Prudent Investor Rule

The American Law Institute in 1992 drafted the Restatement (Third) of Trusts, which revised and superseded the Second Restatement by incorporating modern investment theories and principles. The National Conference of Commissioners on Uniform State Laws incorporated the

Prudent Investor Rule into the Uniform Prudent Investor Act (UPIA) in 1994.

Where previous versions had attempted to make trust assets productive by seeking the highest income possible while preserving the nominal value of principal, the Prudent Investor Act established five principles of prudence.

1. The standard of prudence is applied to any investment as part of the total portfolio, rather than to individual investments. In the trust setting the term "portfolio" embraces all the trust's assets.
2. The tradeoff in all investing between risk and return is identified as the fiduciary's central consideration.
3. The trustee can invest in anything that plays an appropriate role in achieving the risk/return objectives of the trust and that meets the other requirements of prudent investing.
4. The long familiar requirement that fiduciaries diversify their investments has been integrated into the definition of prudent investing.
5. The trustee may delegate investment and management functions, subject to safeguards.

Fiduciary Responsibility

The fundamental, underlying goal of the Prudent Man Rule and its evolution through the years, demonstrated in the development of the UPIA, is to give investors who rely on professional advisors the best opportunity for a successful experience. Mutual funds that implement Investing 3.0 have been more effective at meeting these standards than index funds, which appear attractive because of their low operating expense ratios.

The Future

The Prudent Man Rule continues to evolve with the growing body of knowledge that underlies Modern Portfolio Theory. Out-of-date investment concepts have been replaced with modern investment theory that has transformed the investment industry. Investment research has led to the development of tools and mutual funds that help fiduciaries minimize uncompensated risk and more effectively target a balance between risk and expected return.

Professional advisors who move beyond indexing to Investing 3.0 understand these developments and incorporate their understanding into their prudent investment process. In doing so, they serve the best interests of those they advise.

APPENDIX C

Significant Advances in Investment Theory: 1952 to Present

1952 Harry Markowitz   Nobel Prize–1990
    Diversification and Portfolio Risk
    Diversification reduces risk. Assets evaluated not by individual characteristics but by their effect on a portfolio. An optimal portfolio can be constructed to maximize return for a given standard deviation.

1958 James Tobin   Nobel Prize–1981
    Role of Stocks
    Shifts focus from security selection to portfolio structure. Portfolio of risky assets are formed. Risk is tempered by lending and borrowing.

1961 Merton Miller & Franco Modigliani Nobel Prize–1985 and 1990
    Investments and Capital Structure
    Theorem relating corporate finance to returns. A firm's value is unrelated to its dividend policy. Dividend policy is an unreliable guide for stock selection.

1964   William Sharpe   Nobel Prize–1990
        Single Factor Asset Pricing Risk/Return Model
        Capital Asset Pricing Model. (CAPM) A stock's expected re-
        turn is proportional to the stock's covariance with the overall
        market.

1965   Paul Samuelson   Nobel Prize–1970
        Behavior of Securities Prices
        Market prices are the best estimates of value. Price changes fol-
        low random patterns. Future share prices are unpredictable.

1966   Eugene F. Fama   Nobel Prize–2013
        Efficient Markets Hypothesis
        Security prices reflect values and information accurately and
        quickly. It is difficult, if not impossible, to capture returns in
        excess of market returns without taking greater than market
        levels of risk.

1968   Michael Jensen
        First Major Study of Mutual Fund Performance
        First study of mutual funds indicates active managers un-
        derperform indices. First study of institutional plans (A.G.
        Becker Corp.) indicates active managers underperform indi-
        ces. Becker Corp. gives rise to consulting industry with cre-
        ation of "Green Book" performance tables comparing results
        to benchmarks.

1971   John McQuown, Wells Fargo Bank
        First passive index fund for Samsonite Luggage Company pen-
        sion plan

1972   Fischer Black, Robert Merton, Myron Scholes   Nobel Prize–1997
        Options Pricing Model
        The development of the Options Pricing Model allows new
        ways to segment, quantify, and manage risk. The model spurs
        the development of a market for alternative investments.

1977   Roger Ibbotson and Rex Sinquefield
Database of Securities Prices since 1926
An extensive returns database for multiple asset classes is developed and will become one of the most widely used investment databases. The first extensive, empirical basis for making asset allocation decisions changes the way investors build portfolios.

1981   Rolf Banz
The Size Effect
Analysis of NYSE stocks (1926 – 1975) finds that, in the long term, small companies have higher expected returns than large companies and behave differently.

1984   Eugene F. Fama
Variable Maturity Strategy Implemented
A method of shifting maturities that identifies optimal positions on the fixed-income yield curve without predicting interest rates.

1993   Eugene Fama and Kenneth French
Multifactor Pricing Model and Value Effect
Improves on the single-factor asset pricing model (CAPM). Identifies market, size, and "value" factors in return and develops the three-factor asset pricing model for asset allocation and portfolio analysis.

1995   Steven L. Heston, K. Geert Rouwenhorst, and Roberto E. Wessels
International Size Effect
Finds evidence of higher average returns for small companies in twelve international markets.

1997   United States Treasury
Inflation Protected Bonds
The Treasury conducts the first auction of Treasury Inflation-Protected Securities (TIPS), thus allowing US investors to invest for long periods with minimal default and inflation risk.

2002   National Association of Securities Dealers (NASD)
        Improved Bond Market Transparency
        National Association of Securities Dealers (NASD) introduces
        Trade Reporting and Compliance Engine (TRACE), which re-
        quires the reporting of U.S. corporate bond trades. This data
        greatly improved transparency in the corporate bond market
        and allows researchers to study trading costs in the U.S. corpo-
        rate bond market.

2012   Eugene F. Fama, Kenneth R. French, and Robert Novy-Marx
        Profitability Factor
        Identifies profitability as a new dimension of expected returns.

GLOSSARY

Asset class   A group of securities that exhibits similar characteristics behaves similarly in the marketplace and is subject to the same laws and regulations.

Benchmark   A point of reference used to compare things, for example performance in the investment markets. For example, the S&P 500 is often used as a benchmark.

Bid/ask spread   The difference between the highest price that a buyer is willing to pay for an asset (the bid) and the lowest price a seller is willing to accept to sell it (the ask).

Bloomberg machine   A computer software system that enables investment professionals to monitor and analyze real-time financial market data.

Bonds   A debt investment that pays the investor over a defined period of time at a variable or fixed interest rate.

Collateralized debt obligation (CDO)   A contract to receive payments of interest and principal based on a collection (pool) of debt obligations, such as mortgages and other loans.

Common stock   A security that represents ownership in a corporation.

Coupon rate   The annual coupon payments (interest) paid by the issuer relative to the bond's face (par) value.

Dalbar   An independent rating agency, similar to JD Power, that specializes in investment products and financial service providers.

Dividends   A distribution of a portion of a company's earnings to its shareholders.

Equity risk premium   The excess return that investing in the stock market provides over a risk-free rate, such as the return from government treasury bonds.

ETF	An abbreviation for "exchange-traded fund," which is a closed-end type of mutual fund. ETFs are marketable securities that track an index of stocks, bonds, or a mix of stocks and bonds. Unlike shares of other closed-end funds, the supply of ETF shares is regulated through a mechanism known as creation and redemption, which involves a few large specialized investors, who are the authorized participants (APs).
Exchange	Another name for a marketplace. A finance exchange involves the trading of securities, commodities, derivatives, and other financial instruments.
Fiduciary	A person or organization that owes to another the duty to act in the other's best interests with good faith and trust. It is the highest legal duty of one party to another; it also involves being bound ethically.
Financial capital	The economic resource needed by businesses.
Forecasting	Attempting to predict the future, in this case, the direction of an individual investment, a market, or the economy as a whole.
Fundamental values	The qualitative and quantitative information that contributes to the economic well-being and the subsequent financial health of a company, security, or currency.
Growth companies	Companies that are growing rapidly in comparison to others in their field or to the economy as a whole. They are often associated with higher prices for their stock relative to the information reported in their financial statements.
Index funds	Mutual funds that attempt to replicate the performance of a market index.
Investment markets	A place where investors buy and sell shares of publicly traded securities.

Investment returns	A performance measure used to evaluate the efficiency of an investment or to compare the efficiency of different investments.
Laddered maturities	A portfolio of fixed-income securities (bonds) in which each security has a different maturity date.
Large cap stocks	A company whose market capitalization (number of shares outstanding times price per share) exceeds the market average, such as $5 billion.
Leverage	The amount of debt that a company assumes to buy more assets.
Liquidity	The availability of cash and other immediately spendable assets.
Market prices	The current price for which an investment security can be bought or sold.
Morningstar	An investment research firm that publishes a comprehensive analysis of mutual funds and other investment securities.
Mortgage-backed securities	A type of asset-backed security that is secured by a mortgage or collection of mortgages.
Mutual funds	An investment vehicle made up of a pool of funds collected from many investors for the purpose of investing in securities, such as stocks, bonds, money market instruments, and similar assets.
New York Stock Exchange	The oldest stock exchange in the United States; it is located on Wall Street in lower Manhattan.
Performance	The return on an investment portfolio.
Preferred stock	Stock that entitles the holder to a fixed dividend, whose payment takes priority over that of common-stock dividends.
Present value	The current worth of a future sum of money or stream of cash flows given a specified rate of return.
Private sector	Businesses not owned or operated by the government.

Ratings agencies	A company that provides investors with assessments of an investment's risk.
SEC	The Securities and Exchange Commission is a U.S. government agency that oversees securities transactions, the activities of financial professionals, and trading of mutual funds.
Sector	A subset of the investment market that shares similar characteristics. Sometimes it refers to individual securities grouped by industry or a group of similar industries.
Share	A unit of ownership interest in a corporation or financial asset.
Short	Selling securities you do not own under a contract that requires you to purchase them, covering the sale later at an agreed upon price. Short sellers profit when the price drops below the agreed upon price and lose when the price rises. Short selling is speculative and very risky.
Subprime mortgages	A type of mortgage normally issued by a lending institution to borrowers with low credit ratings.
Success ratio	The percentage of a mutual fund's reported performance realized by its investors.
Tracking error	The difference between a portfolio's returns and the benchmark it was meant to mimic or beat.
Treasury bills	A short-term debt obligation backed by the U.S. government with a maturity of less than one year.
Turnover	Portfolio turnover is a measure of how frequently assets within a fund are bought and sold by the managers.
Valuation	The process of determining a security's current worth.
Yield curve	A line that plots the interest rates—at a set point in time—of bonds with equal credit quality but differing maturity dates.

ENDNOTES

1. "Chapter 1: Markets," *Morningstar Indexes Yearbook* (2005), 3.

2. Leonard Read, "I, Pencil: My Family Tree as Told to Leonard E. Read," *The Freeman*, December 1958.

3. In 2015, the daily average for world equity trading was 98.6 million trades involving $447.3 billion.

4. Kenneth French is the Roth Family Distinguished Professor of Finance at the Tuck School of Business, Dartmouth College, and director and head of investment policy for Dimensional Fund Advisors.

5. Ali Kabiri, "'Theory anchors' explain the 1920s NYSE Bubble," *London School of Economics Financial Markets Group,* Special Paper Series, vol. 218 (London: Financial Markets Group Research Centre, London School of Economics and Political Science, 2013), 1.

6. Kabiri, 4.

7. Alan Greenspan, in a speech, "The Challenge of Central Banking in a Democratic Society," given at the American Enterprise Institute on December 5, 1996, retrieved from https://en.wikipedia.org/wiki/Irrational_exuberance.

8. Benjamin Graham and David Dodd, *Security Analysis* (New York: McGraw-Hill, 1934).

9. John Burr Williams Jr., *The Theory of Investment Value* (Cambridge, Mass.: Harvard University Press, 1938).

10. C2VTrader.com, "The Standard & Poor's 500 Index," retrieved from www.c2vtrader.com/S&P-500.php.

11. Gerald M. Loeb, *The Battle for Investment Survival* (New York: John Wiley & Sons, 1935).

12. I saw this firsthand when I joined Rosenberg Real Estate Equity Funds (RREEF). We were set up exclusively to capture pension investments in income-producing real estate. While at RREEF, I helped launch the National Council of Real Estate Investment Fiduciaries (NCREIF), which I named to sound like RREEF, to track the performance of these real estate investments.

13. Eugene Fama and Kenneth French, "Luck Versus Skill in the Cross-Section of Mutual Fund Returns," *Journal of Finance*, October 2010.

14. Andrew Ang, William Goetzmann, and Stephen Schaefer, *Evaluation of Active Management of the Norwegian Government Pension Fund—Global* (December 14, 2009).

15. Diane Mulcahy, Bill Weeks, and Harold Bradley, *"We Have Met the Enemy . . . And He Is Us," Lessons from Twenty Years of the Kauffman Foundation's Investments in Venture Capital Funds and The Triumph of Hope over Experience* (May 2012).

16. "A Conversation with Benjamin Graham," *Financial Analysts Journal* (September–October, 1976).

17. Peter Lynch, *Beating the Street* (New York: Simon & Schuster, 1993), 60.

18. Eugene Fama, *Random Walks in Stock-Market Prices,* Selected Papers No. 16, (Chicago: Graduate School of Business, University of Chicago, 1965).

19. Burton Malkiel, *A Random Walk Down Wall Street* (New York: W. W. Norton, 1973), 246.

20. Merton Miller, *Investment Gurus* (New York: Simon & Schuster, 1997).

21. Eugene Fama and Kenneth French, "Luck Versus Skill in the Cross-Section of Mutual Fund Returns," *Journal of Finance* (October 2010).

22. *Business Week*, August 13, 1979.

23. *Fortune*, September 28, 1998.

24. *Money*, August 2012.

25. Dalbar, *Dalbar's 22nd Annual Quantitative Analysis of Investor Behavior*, 3.

26. John C. Bogle, *The Economics of the Mutual Fund Industry: For Fund Investors . . . for Fund Managers*, (October 5, 1999), 8.

27. Merton Miller, Investment Gurus (New York: Simon & Schuster, 1997).

28. H. M. Markowitz, "Portfolio Selection," *The Journal of Finance*, vol. 7 no. 1 (March 1952): 77–91.

29. William F. Sharpe, Nobel Prize in Economic Sciences, 1990.

30. Kate Ancell, "The Origin of the First Index Fund," *The University of Chicago Booth School of Business* (March 28, 2012): 4.

31. Ancell, "The Origin," 12.

32. Ancell, "The Origin," 12.

33. John C. Bogle, *The First Index Mutual Fund: A History of Vanguard Index Trust and the Vanguard Index Strategy*, 1997, retrieved from https://www.vanguard.com/bogle_site/lib/sp19970401.html.

34. Ancell, "The Origin," 14–15.

35. Bogle, *Economics of the Mutual Fund Industry,* 8.

36. Bogle, *Economics of the Mutual Fund Industry,* 8.

37. *Morningstar Indexes Yearbook* (2005), 3.

38. Rolf W. Banz, "The Relationship between Return and Market Value of Common Stocks," *Journal of Financial Economics,* vol. 9 no. 1 (1981): 3–18.

39. Eugene Fama and Kenneth French, "Common Risk Factors in the Returns on Stocks and Bonds, *Journal of Financial Economics,* vol. 33 (1993): 3–56.

40. Robert Novy-Marx, "The Other Side of Value: The Gross Profitability Premium," Research paper, Simon Graduate School of Business, University of Rochester (June 2012).

41. Eugene F. Fama, *Journal of Financial Economics,* vol. 13 no. 4 (1984): 509–28.

42. Francis M. Kinniry Jr., Colleen M. Jaconetti, Michael A. DiJoseph, and Yan Zilbering, "Putting a Value on Your Value: Quantifying Vanguard Advisor's Alpha," *Vanguard Research* (March 2014).

43. John J. Bowen Jr., "The Wealth Management Edge," *CEG Worldwide* (2012): 113.

44. John C. Bogle, *The Economics of the Mutual Fund Industry: For Fund Investors . . . for Fund Managers,* (October 5, 1999), 8.

45. Dalbar, *Dalbar's 22 nd Annual Quantitative Analysis of Investor Behavior,* 5.

46. John C. Bogle, *The Economics of the Mutual Fund Industry: For Fund Investors . . . for Fund Managers*, (October 5, 1999), 8.

47. *Morningstar Indexes Yearbook* (2005), 3.

48. *Morningstar Indexes Yearbook* (2005), 3.

49. *Morningstar Indexes Yearbook* (2005), 3.

About the Author

Rick Raybin has forty years of experience in the financial industry. He holds a BA in economics from Bowdoin College and an MBA in finance and accounting from Columbia University. He worked as a certified public accountant for Coopers and Lybrand before becoming CFO of Rosenberg Real Estate Equity Funds. In that position, he teamed up with major US banks and insurance companies to form the National Council of Real Estate Investment Fiduciaries, and he served as its first president and chairman. He currently works as a financial advisor.

Rick lives in San Mateo, California with his wife, Ramona. He has four adult children. His interests include tennis and amateur theater. He also volunteers with community organizations, often serving as treasurer and advising on endowment investment strategies.

Made in the USA
Columbia, SC
21 May 2019